CHARACTER

TRI◐◐S

*Each TRIOS book
addresses an important
theme in critical theory,
philosophy, or cultural
studies through three
extended essays written
in close collaboration by
leading scholars.*

CHARACTER

THREE INQUIRIES
IN LITERARY STUDIES

AMANDA
Anderson

RITA
Felski

TORIL
Moi

The University of Chicago Press
Chicago and London

The University of Chicago Press, Chicago 60637
The University of Chicago Press, Ltd., London
© 2019 by The University of Chicago
Published 2019
Printed in the United States of America

28 27 26 25 24 23 22 21 20 19   1 2 3 4 5

ISBN-13: 978-0-226-65852-0 (cloth)
ISBN-13: 978-0-226-65866-7 (paper)
ISBN-13: 978-0-226-65883-4 (e-book)
DOI: https://doi.org/10.7208/chicago/9780226658834.001.0001

Library of Congress Cataloging-in-Publication Data

Names: Container of (work): Anderson, Amanda, 1960– Thinking with
    character. | Container of (work): Moi, Toril. Rethinking character. |
    Container of (work): Felski, Rita, 1956– Identifying with characters.
Title: Character : three inquiries in literary studies / Amanda Anderson, Rita
    Felski, and Toril Moi.
Other titles: Trios (Chicago, Ill.)
Description: Chicago ; London : The University of Chicago Press, 2019. |
    Series: Trios
Identifiers: LCCN 2019017471 | ISBN 9780226658520 (cloth : alk. paper) |
    ISBN 9780226658667 (pbk. : alk. paper) | ISBN 9780226658834 (e-book)
Subjects: LCSH: Characters and characteristics in literature. | Literature—
    History and criticism—Theory, etc.
Classification: LCC PN56.4.C48 2019 | DDC 809/.927—dc23
LC record available at https://lccn.loc.gov/2019017471

CONTENTS

INTRODUCTION

Amanda Anderson, Rita Felski,
and Toril Moi

This book is a contribution to the current reassessment of character in literary studies. We consider recent developments within the field as well as the longer history of academic practices that have shaped—and often constrained—views of character. Our aim is to explore the possibilities that are opened up by thinking about characters in new ways. Individual chapters consider the taboo on treating characters as if they were real people, what it means to identify with characters, and the experience of thinking with characters.

Our essays do not look at character in isolation from other formal, thematic, and social concerns, nor do they attempt to develop a general theory of character that can be applied to an infinite range of examples. Given the variability of characters and the fictional worlds they inhabit, as mediated by genre, medium, style, and form, as well as the differing expectations and interpretive schemas of audiences, any such ambition strikes us as misplaced. At the same time, we see our focus on character as being implicated in—and having implications for—larger questions about the aims and practices of criticism. Concern with character is a defining aspect of reader or viewer engagement with many forms of fiction. It is one of the means by which fiction makes claims upon us. Yet criticism has often failed to give this concern its full due, demoting character to little more than an effect of linguistic, political, or—most recently—psychological structures. Contemporary scholars in the humanities, as Robert Pippin remarks, are adept at third-person analysis of texts—explaining why certain features have come to exist and what functions they serve—while resolutely avoiding first-person or normative questions: why these texts matter, or might matter, to us.[1]

This book continues and extends lines of inquiry that we have developed in our recent work. In *Revolution of the Ordinary: Literary Studies after Wittgenstein, Austin, and Cavell*, Toril Moi shows that Wittgenstein's vision of language provides a starting point for rethinking fundamental questions in literary theory. In *Uses of Literature* and *The Limits of Critique*, Rita Felski explores alternatives to a hermeneutics of suspicion, arguing for approaches that can acknowledge the varied and often unpredictable uses of literature by lay as well as academic readers. Extending her longstanding interest in character and ethos as intrinsic features of both theoretical and literary practice, Amanda Anderson argues in *Psyche and Ethos: Moral Life after Psychology* for the importance of finding an adequate vocabulary and set of interpretive methods with which to capture literature's exploration of the moral life, especially in light of the increasing power of psychological and scientific explanations of human action.[2]

Despite our different intellectual commitments, we share a dissatisfaction with the frameworks that have dominated literary studies over the last few decades. Our focus on character allows several key issues to come to the fore. We are all interested, for example, in how fiction connects to ordinary life and the responses of lay as well as academic audiences. We are inclined to treat works of fiction as potential sources of insight rather than as examples of unknowingness or complicity that need to be corrected by a theoretical metalanguage. We are interested in undoing conventionally formalist approaches to literary form. And while we share a strong interest in fiction's ties to ethical and political life, we do not subscribe to the assumptions of a "textual politics" that automatically correlates literary form to a troubling of norms or subverting of dominant ideologies. Rather, we are interested in clearing the ground for new attempts to understand characters and the claims they make on their readers.

In the remainder of this introduction we review the domains of scholarship pertinent to a renewed consideration of character, aiming to acknowledge both the contributions and the constraints of frameworks in literary theory, historical criticism, the field of philosophy and literature, and newer approaches in cognitive science. A central thread in our discussion is that understandings of character have long been shaped by specific critical norms that arose with the professionalization of literary studies and continued into the era of New Criticism, poststructuralism, ideological criticism, and cognitive literary studies, and that these norms are ripe for reassessment. We map this influence and specify in a preliminary way how we view our own contributions to the developing debate over character.

In *Structuralist Poetics*, Jonathan Culler noted that French postwar writers had been highly critical of the kind of realism practiced by their great predecessor Honoré de Balzac. In their own work, the new writers—writers such as Nathalie Sarraute, Alain Robbe-Grillet, Claude Simon, and Philippe Sollers— treated character very differently. To them, a character was not a portrait of a human being but a node in a textual network. Culler calls such characters "pronominal heroes" to convey that for these authors character was an effect of writing (in this case of personal pronouns).[3] Meanwhile, theorists of structuralism in France were as critical toward nineteenth-century realism as their colleagues the novelists. (Indeed, often the novelists were also the theorists.) As a result, most structuralists paid little attention to character. But some did. Building on Vladimir Propp's work, they tended to see character solely as a function of action. From a corpus of Russian folktales, Propp distilled seven such roles: the hero, the helper, the villain, the false hero, the donor,

[right margin, handwritten] centrally connecting point

[left margin, handwritten] relating/serving as pronoun

the sought-for person (often the princess), and her father. In France, the Lithuanian-born Algirdas Greimas and the Bulgarian émigré Tzvetan Todorov further synthesized these narrative roles, but they too considered characters not as psychological or moral beings but as narrative actants, textual constraints, or effects of interconnections in the textual weave. For Roland Barthes, for example, character was an illusion of individuality created by the proper name.[4] Culler himself suggested that we consider character as a convention—a reiteration and variation on a stock figure or a stereotype. Character is based not on real life but on "cultural models."[5] These theories succeeded in their wish to avoid concepts such as the autonomous subject, the human, or reference to reality, but at the cost of leaving us with nothing to say about characters as objects of identification, sources of emotional response, or agents of moral vision and behavior.

A more recent generation of narratologists builds on the formalist tradition but raises questions which move the study of character into new arenas. Fictional characters, they point out, are not just effects of language but possess a relatively independent status that allows them to move freely across genres and media. Uri Margolin, for example, argues that "character is a general semiotic element, independent of any particular verbal expression and ontologically different from it."[6] These scholars agree that characters are entities that exist within fictional worlds, but they disagree about their ontological status: what is the precise nature of character and how exactly are these fictional worlds to be understood? An important philosophical source of inspiration for this strand of literary theory is Kendall Walton's theory of make-believe worlds.[7] Fotis Jannidis offers a helpful delineation of the salient differences between narratologists on these questions. He distinguishes between philosophically inflected discussions of possible-world theories, as in the work of Margolin; the use of cognitive science to conceive of characters as mental models created by readers, by Ralf Schneider, for example; and his own prioritizing of the text as an intentional object in a manner that he describes as "neo-hermeneutical." We find it revealing, however, that Jannidis begins his essay by noting that "most theoretical approaches to character seek to circumscribe reliance on real-world knowledge in some way and to treat characters as entities in a storyworld subject to specific rules."[8] Given our commitment to building on the variety and complexity of ordinary response to fictional characters, we are not inclined to draw such strict boundaries between "real-world" and "story-world" knowledge and rules.

A different revision of the formalist tradition can be found in two seminal books: Alex Woloch's *The One vs. the Many: Minor Characters and the Space of the Protagonist in the Novel* (2003) and John Frow's *Character and Person* (2014). Woloch was one of the first to recognize that the taboo on "treating characters as if they were real people" placed undesirable restrictions on literary critics. Although he doesn't reject outright the claim that discussions of character are doomed to be naively realist, he recognizes that literary studies has lost the art of discussing characters in illuminating ways and that critics simply have to find ways to acknowledge the "implied resemblance" between the character and the human being.[9] Seeking to produce a new synthesis, Woloch sets out a critical procedure capable of uniting discussions of the human aspects of characters with the formalist understanding of narrative structure. To do so, he proposes that critics study "the dynamic flux of attention" given to different characters in and by the narrative structure.[10] Introducing the concepts of "character-space" and "character-system," Woloch wishes to account for the human as well as the formal aspects of character. The character-space is the "particular and charged encounter between an individual human personality and a determined space and position within the narrative as a whole"; the character-system is the "arrangement of multiple and differentiated character-spaces . . . into a unified narrative structure."[11] Woloch's study of character-spaces and character-systems in *Pride and Prejudice*, *Great Expectations*, and *Le Père Goriot* powerfully contributed to putting the discussion of character back on the critical agenda.

John Frow's *Character and Person* has the ambitious aim of producing a theory which can account for both character and persons across different media. He begins by declaring that characters are "ontological hybrids," at once "person-like entities" and "pieces of writing and imaging."[12] A self-declared formalist, Frow acknowledges that critics need to be able to discuss characters, including our identification with them and our emotional responses to them. The problem is that usually such discussions are carried on in a language that sounds "humanist" or, as he puts it, "ethical." The goal, for Frow, is to produce a theory, a language, that accounts both for the "concept of fictional character" and for the "category of the human person itself."[13] Only such a theory will enable us to discuss phenomena such as identification, emotional response, and so on in adequate ways. Thus, Frow is suspicious of any kind of formulation that implies, however fleetingly, that "the quasi-persons of narrative [are] somehow extricable from the text in which they fully exist."[14] We agree that readers and critics remain aware of the fictional status of characters even as they invest in them in various ways. But Frow's uncompromising formalism and his antipathy to moral frameworks create interpretive strictures that are at odds with our own projects in this book. Nonetheless, the importance of his intervention is such that we spend considerable time discussing his views (see the contributions by Toril Moi and Amanda Anderson).

Historical studies of the novel have tended to subordinate questions of character, either literary or moral, to larger narratives about the genre's rise and especially its central role in modernity. In these narratives, from Lukács's *The Theory of the Novel* to Ian Watt's *The Rise of the Novel* to Nancy Armstrong's *Desire and Domestic Fiction*, the main interest lies in the modern individual, whether that individual bears the burden of modern homelessness (Lukács), represents a form of particularity and individuality tied to the emergence of empiricism and bourgeois economic life (Watt), or expresses the subject-constituting force of modern disciplinary power (Armstrong).[15] Studies that have focused more specifically on the formal qualities of characters, and on readers' relations to them, have largely done so within the frame of an economic reading of modernity, especially in work on the eighteenth-century novel. Discussions of characters within these studies are often vibrant and compelling, attesting to an abiding interest in the forms of life represented in fiction, yet the overall theoretical framework tends to privilege the rise of bourgeois modernity, the estranging effects of the credit economy, and emergent forms of discipline and self-fashioning that new economic conditions both effected and prompted.

Catherine Gallagher's *Nobody's Story*, for example, explores the effect of the credit economy on writers and readers, showing that it accorded a knowing agency to women writers at the same time as it placed the emergence of fictional forms and fictional characters within a broader cultural formation in which economic structures shaped new forms of (impersonal) identity.[16] Deidre Shauna Lynch's *The Economy of Character* seeks to demystify a notion of character understood apart from market-driven desires and forms of self-expression, embracing the mutual imbrication of inner life and socially embedded desires.[17] We acknowledge the powerful contribution of these studies but are ourselves interested in how a more capacious acknowledgment of readerly interest in characters might prompt other forms of critical engagement, ones that recognize our responses to characters not only as situated within ideological and sociohistorical contexts but also as importantly moral and affective in ways that much of the historical work in the field has left unexplored.

Work in the arena of philosophy and literature gives more emphasis to these questions in its unabashed use of characters to exemplify instructive forms of response to the conditions of human existence or the demands of moral life. Martha Nussbaum, in *Love's Knowledge*, uses novelistic scenes of sympathy between characters to show the importance of affective knowledge, advancing the idea that literature in particular has a key role to play in the larger social and cultural process of moral education.[18] In *Contingency, Irony, and Solidarity*, Richard Rorty shows how literary works can increase our sensitivity to cruelty and so advance our capacity to avoid causing harm.[19] Stanley Cavell's work has focused on the ways in which literature and film explore dramas of skepticism and acknowledgment. Skepticism marks the attitude in which dependency on others, and on a shared world, is disavowed. Forms of acknowledgment and repair, by contrast, signal moments of moral achievement in which characters and/or authors counteract the movement toward skepticism and withdrawal from the world.[20] Robert Pippin, in *Henry James and Modern Moral Life*, reads James "with the grain" in order to draw out his distinctive moral thinking in the face of modern conditions, within a highly sensitive understanding of anxieties about dependency.[21] These works unanxiously accord a centrality to character and are in this way productively unconstrained by the field conditions of literary studies. For this very reason, however, this scholarship has had limited influence on literary-critical approaches to character. We hope through our essays to broach more directly the formal and theoretical questions raised by a sustained focus on character, within the broader context of the history of criticism over the past several decades.

Some influential recent approaches fall under the broad umbrella of cognitive studies or cognitive psychology, where the shared feature is an interest in linking analyses of literature or film to the investigation of mental processing. "Cognitive" is a potentially misleading adjective, however, insofar as the emotional aspects of response often play an important part in these accounts. Murray Smith's *Engaging Character*, for example, makes a case for the saliency of character in viewers' emotional

engagement with film. Characters, he argues, are not ade-
quately understood as textual effects or ideological symptoms
but are fictional analogues of human agents: person schemas
that play a vital role in triggering viewer involvement.[22] Marco
Caracciolo draws on cognitive psychology as well as phenomenology to examine how readers assign meaning to literary
characters. Focusing on contemporary examples of "strange"
first-person narrators, he seeks to capture the experiential dynamics of reader engagement with character as a shifting blend
of involvement and distance.[23] And Alan Palmer proposes that
literary analysis of fictional characters would benefit from
drawing on research in neuroscience as well as psychology. We
are drawn into story worlds, he argues, by a desire to track the
workings of the fictional minds contained within them that is
not dissimilar to our interest in the minds of those around us.[24]

Other forms of research along these general lines turn to the
field of evolutionary psychology. Lisa Zunshine, for example,
contends that fiction trains a capacity in mind reading: the ability to decipher the inner states of characters from textual cues.[25]
In reacting to characters, readers draw on a "theory of mind"
that has evolved in humans to help promote forms of social co-
operation. Blakey Vermeule also suggests that attachments to
characters can be explained only by analogy to our ties to real
persons. Fiction helps cultivate a "Machiavellian intelligence"
that offers an evolutionary advantage in allowing us to navigate
the complexities and subtleties of interpersonal interactions.[26]
We find these engagements with cognitive science thought-
provoking, but we have reservations about approaches that too
narrowly conceive of the practices and motivations of reading,
especially when they proceed via an informing assumption of
humans as fundamentally self-interested or always seeking to
maximize their political advantage.

Our own contributions issue from a set of overlapping commitments and cautions. One topic that concerns us is the relationship between literary scholars and nonacademic readers, a

relationship often portrayed as a dichotomy. In their efforts to gain an institutional foothold and demonstrate the legitimacy of literary studies as a discipline, scholars of literature in the early twentieth century felt impelled to underscore the difference between their own practices of interpretation and everyday forms of reading. This difference was consolidated by the New Critics, who, as is often noted, defined their dispassionate analysis of literary works against the more emotional and impressionistic responses of nonacademic readers. The transformation of literary studies over the last half century, for the most part, further accentuated this divide. The new political and philosophical frameworks seized on by literary critics were premised on an ingrained suspicion of everyday assumptions and common beliefs. Widely used academic methods of interpretation assumed a division between the obvious or surface meaning of a text and a hidden or counterintuitive meaning that revealed itself only to the expert reader. Theorists of character, meanwhile, were careful to distinguish their own approaches from the "naive" perspectives of ordinary readers.

This dichotomy is now being reassessed, for reasons that are both intellectual (a rethinking of the techniques of demystification) and institutional (the decreased enrollments and plummeting prestige of literary studies inspire a new concern with building bridges to wider publics). Cultural studies, of course, has long argued for taking the concerns of ordinary readers seriously—for example, in groundbreaking works by Ien Ang and Janice Radway.[27] A similar concern is now beginning to manifest itself in the mainstream of literary studies. Rachel Buurma and Laura Heffernan, however, portray this interest in a skeptical light. "A new figure beckons to the literary critic: the figure of the common reader," they write. "Her authority derives from her lack of credentials; neither scholar nor critic, student nor expert, she is defined largely by her undisciplinary and undisciplined reading practices."[28] Surveying recent accounts of this reader, they describe her as a mascot, muse, or model for critics trying to wriggle free of the straitjacket of scholarship. Such a figure, they suggest, is little more than a fetish or a fantasy: a romanticized image that reveals more about the existential crises of critics than about readers themselves. Having fallen out of love with their discipline, critics are now cathecting onto a nostalgic idea of the common reader—as symbolizing a more authentic relationship to literature—in the vain hope of escaping their own status as professionals. This argument gets things backward. The figure of the ordinary or nonacademic reader ("common reader" is a phrase now rarely used) is not just a trope invented by critics to convey their own sense of professional anomie. Most critics do not live in academic enclaves, cut off from all contact with the outside world; their experiences overlap with those of nonacademic audiences at numerous points. Literary scholars were, after all, once ordinary readers; we all retain memories and mental traces, whether hazy or vivid, of what it feels like to read for absorption and self-loss. (Some of us continue to read in this way, without embarrassment, when we are off duty; professional training does not determine all aspects of one's being in the world.) And we routinely engage with the assumptions and attitudes of ordinary readers in the classroom, interacting with undergraduates who are not yet familiar with advanced techniques of interpretation. Finally, many of us have friends or family members who have never quite grasped what we do for a living and who are happily ignorant of Cleanth Brooks or Julia Kristeva but who participate in book clubs or line up for hours to get an autograph from Stephen King. The interest in ordinary readers is not a puzzling new fashion that requires decryption—such readers are a backdrop to the lives of many, perhaps most, literary critics.

Meanwhile, none of the critics surveyed by Buurma and Heffernan are advocating that professional critics abandon their training. There are obvious differences between academic criticism and everyday reading, which serve quite different functions and purposes. Studying literature or art or music is not synonymous with the everyday enjoyment of them. The salient issue, however, is whether this difference should be seen as an antithesis—with the skeptical gaze of the scholar puncturing the sentimental illusions and naive attachments of lay audiences. Or whether we might imagine a form of literary studies that engages, explicates, and builds on ordinary response rather than dismissing or demystifying it. (Once past their polemical introduction, Buurma and Heffernan offer a fascinating and informative account of how academic and everyday interests were intertwined in the classrooms of Cleanth Brooks and Edmund Wilson.) That certain kinds of responses to literature are ordinary, in other words, does not mean that we know how to discuss them with the seriousness they deserve.

What, in this light, should we make of the common tendency to treat characters as if they were persons? In contrast to much scholarship on character, we see this tendency not as an error to be corrected but as a fascinating topic to be explored. We are obviously not arguing that characters *are* persons. But in order to discuss characters in interesting ways we often find ourselves using some of the same language we use to talk about real human beings. We may, for example, want to ask about a character's motivations or intentions, or wonder what goes on in a character's head in a specific situation. We may attribute feelings and thoughts to characters. Even highly trained literary critics may find that they sometimes identify with or respond emotionally to characters as if they were persons. This is not to deny, of course, that readers also discuss characters in ways that differ from how we talk about real people. We draw attention to their fabricated or fictional status in various ways: comparing a character in a film to the character in the novel on which the film is based, for example, or saying things like "I was rooting for the heroine until that plot twist at the end made her seem completely unconvincing." There is nothing esoteric or unusual about such remarks; reflecting on the artifactual status of characters is part of everyday response to works of fiction.

We must acknowledge that there is an ingrained suspicion, in some intellectual circles, about any kind of reference to personhood. Doesn't the word imply a commitment to a problematic humanism, to ideologies of individualism that help sustain structures of gender, race, and class inequality? We would respond by questioning the assumption that using the word "person" denotes any particular worldview. Indeed, as our essays attest, the three of us are differently invested in how and why an emphasis on persons and character is important to a renewed literary studies. The word "person" (or "human being" or "people") is open to varied conceptions of what a person is. Words don't come with essences; their meaning is established by their use. One of the more problematic legacies of critical theory, in our view, has been a tendency to encourage leaps from the use of particular words to imputations of "isms," as if any reference to a person implied humanism, as if any reference to presence implied a metaphysics of origin, as if any reference to "women" implied essentialist feminism, and so on. The relation between word use and subscription to particular theories or philosophies is much more contingent and variable than such arguments are inclined to admit.

Nor does our focus on character imply any specific stance on the complex and variegated field of posthumanism. Posthumanism has been a significant and generative force in literary studies and encompasses a wide variety of positions, from animal studies to thing theory and new materialisms. We do not address these fields directly, but we would like to suggest that many of the key elements of our emphasis on character—in particular the importance of stance, attitude, and relationality—are highly relevant to them. On the one hand, posthumanism could be said to carry within it the enduring force of the characterological in its emphasis on the importance of how we relate to the nonhuman world. On the other hand, in characterizing this world, posthumanist thinkers cannot help but impute character to it, enacting various forms of anthropomorphism and animism. In this way, the ethically capacious aspects of posthumanism are potentially continuous with, and not opposed to, a renewed interrogation of character.

Here we might also note that, after the theory revolutions of the 1960s and 1970s, critics often replaced talk of ethics with talk of politics. Questions of the moral good were spurned as individualist and linked to a humanism in need of repudiation; questions of politics, by contrast, were seen as structural and therefore compatible with radical challenges to subjectivity. The idea that ethical approaches to literature must be individualist and humanist has been difficult to dislodge. As late as 2014, John Frow distinguished between "ethical" critics, who consider that "characters are to be treated as though they were persons," and "structuralist" critics, for whom "characters are to be treated purely as textual constructs."[29]

To be sure, ethical inquiries drawing on the philosophy of thinkers such as Jacques Derrida, Emmanuel Lévinas, and Giorgio Agamben escaped the general opprobrium. For philosophers and literary critics in this tradition, literature does not hand out ethical instruction but rather undoes knowledge, unsettles expectations, and brings us face-to-face with alterity. In so doing, literature forces us to confront the limitations of our own judgment, our own categories of thought and perception. As Derek Attridge puts it in *The Singularity of Literature*: "The distinctive ethical demand made by the literary work is not to be identified with its characters or its plot, with the human intercourse and judgements it portrays." Instead, "it is to be found in what makes it literature: its staging of the fundamental processes whereby language works upon us and the world."[30]

While we don't disagree that reading some forms of literature may produce unsettling encounters with otherness, we find this line of argument too limited in its reach. Criticism in this vein often focuses entirely on language and form at the expense of character and is unable to grapple with questions about the rightness of judgment and action that often arise in engagement with fiction. Meanwhile, the claim that literature is a source of alterity overlooks the fact that while some forms of writing may challenge or estrange readers, indeed shake them to their very core, other forms of literary expression may be sought out for their familiarity or their consoling power. There is no such thing as "literature as such." The category of "literature" (or "the novel") is too diverse to have one, clearly definable effect.

In a recent essay Nora Hämäläinen shows, in ways that have implications for literary studies, that moral philosophy isn't doomed to simplistic forms of character analysis. Moral philosophers, she argues, use literature in three different ways: thin, thick, and open-ended. In the "thin" use, the moral philosopher paraphrases a scene or a conflict in a novel and uses it as a "case to think about, a test for our intuitions."[31] Here the philosopher isn't really interested in the literary text for its own sake; it is mined for salient examples that can help to bring out one's own arguments more clearly. This common practice has helped to give ethical inquiry a bad reputation in literary studies.

To exemplify "thick" use, Hämäläinen turns to Martha Nussbaum's reading of *Antigone*. In this case, the philosopher "attempts to enter into dialogue with the literary work—with all its complexities, its point of view"—in order to "think better" about moral questions that a "regular argumentative style" fails to bring out in the right way.[32] However, Hämäläinen shows that Nussbaum doesn't let literature upset her own philosophical categories: literature complements, but does not fundamentally challenge, regular forms of philosophical inquiry. Hämäläinen's analysis pinpoints one reason why so many literary critics have kept their distance from Nussbaum's literary readings. At her best, Nussbaum brings out elements in the literary text worth noticing and discussing further. But because she fails to challenge philosophy's way of posing moral questions, her arguments in the end often subordinate literature to philosophy, in ways that literary critics find problematic.

For an example of an "open-ended" use of literature, Hämäläinen cites Cora Diamond's reading of J. M. Coetzee's *The Lives of Animals*. While other philosophers have read Coetzee's text as a treatise on animal rights, Diamond sees it as dealing with the life of a wounded human animal: a woman who doesn't know how to live in a world in which animals are being tortured and eaten.[33] Diamond, Hämäläinen writes, "refuses to cooperate in the act of translation from literature to philosophy, from representation to argument, from experience to explanation."[34] While Nussbaum turns the literary work into an "answer, illustration, or argument," Diamond's reading is a fundamental challenge to the usual procedures of philosophical thought.[35]

This account of what Diamond is doing resonates in some ways, but not others, with the literary-critical stress on defamiliarization and otherness. Diamond doesn't write about "alterity" as such. She raises specific questions about the character Elizabeth Costello. What kind of person is she? How do her existential difficulties challenge philosophy's usual modes of thinking in a world which accepts cruelty toward animals? Such questions don't reduce the text to existing philosophical concerns but rather acknowledge its challenge to those concerns. Diamond's "open-ended" reading of literature relies on a commitment to something we can call moral or philosophical attention. On this point the concerns of the philosopher and those of the literary critic converge. For Diamond, the reader needs to be willing to follow the author on her adventure, to see what is at stake in the work.[36] This spirit of inquiry is one we endorse and hope to encourage.

A final note. Just about all theorists of character take for granted that literary characters are fictional. This leads them to connect the idea of a character with theories of fiction or fictionality and to try to establish the ontological status of fictional characters.[37] But insofar as theories of character are bound up with theories of fictionality, they fail to do justice both to literary nonfiction and to some of the most exciting and important forms of contemporary writing. After all, questions of identification and emotional response are also relevant to nonfictional characters. True-crime writing (such as Truman Capote's *In Cold Blood*), literary biographies, and memoirs all inspire readers to respond to characters. Whether there are significant differences in the response to characters known to be nonfictional deserves further discussion. We also need ways to talk about a new wave of highly visible and widely discussed literary works which strive to undo the divide between fiction and nonfiction. Karl Ove Knausgård's *My Struggle* and Sheila Heti's *How Should a Person Be?* may well be novels, but they are surely not fiction as that term has usually been understood. In this book we can't even begin to do justice to such modes of literary writing. But we can draw attention to their existence and open the way for future investigations.

We turn, now, to an overview of the arguments of individual chapters. In her contribution, Toril Moi asks why literary critics constantly warn their students (and each other) not to treat literary characters as if they were real people. What is at stake in this injunction? How did it come about? Is there any reason to continue insisting on it? The essay analyzes the intellectual and sociological origins of the taboo and examines the most recent attempt to theorize it. Overall, Moi argues that the taboo came into being as part of an attempt to turn literary criticism into a genuine academic pursuit aligned with the formalist aesthetics of modernism, the cutting-edge literary movement of the pre-war era. The result was a new, professional criticism that took modernism's understanding of form to be axiomatic, fundamental to its very existence.

After World War II, the same fundamental "modernist formalism" came to be generally shared by critics who otherwise differed in their priorities. To be a professional literary critic simply was to be an expert on form, as against students and laypeople who persisted in talking about content and character. This was as true for self-proclaimed historicists as for self-proclaimed formalists. But today, the aesthetic and intellectual situation has changed. The old theoretical paradigms are exhausted. New kinds of literary writing break up the old boundary between fiction and nonfiction, depart from traditional modernist conventions, and thus present critics with new challenges.

Moi begins by examining L. C. Knights's 1933 essay *How Many Children Had Lady Macbeth?* with a view to laying bare its conditions of possibility, beginning with its literary and aesthetic investments. But she also considers it from the point of view of the sociology of intellectuals. She shows that Knights's distaste for "character talk" is not so much a theoretical or philosophical analysis of the question of character as an expression of his situation as an ambitious young critic eager to promote a new, professional, academic literary criticism capable of doing justice to modernism.

The "modernist-formalist" alliance that fueled Knights's intellectual passion dominated literary studies for two generations. But whereas Knights was promoting a certain critical practice, a later generation of critics turned the taboo into theoretical dogma. After World War II, the prohibition on treating characters as if they were real people became a foundational axiom for literary studies. At the turn of the century, there were signs that critics wished to be able to do more with characters than just insist that they were textual entities, mere patterns of signification. Alex Woloch's 2003 book *The One vs. the Many* was the first to try to transcend the old taboo, not so much by rejecting it as by incorporating it in a new synthesis.

Moi ends her essay by analyzing John Frow's theory of characters as "ontological hybrids" in his magisterial 2014 book *Character and Person*. On Moi's analysis, Frow, who explicitly declares himself to be a formalist, demonstrates how the traditional way of doing theory turns what once was a set of specific, historically situated professional and aesthetic commitments into an ahistorical ontology. Drawing on Wittgenstein's analysis of the problems incurred by the usual attempts to "theorize" (to define a phenomenon so as to bring it under a concept), she shows that in the case of literary characters, such efforts don't work. At the end of the theorization we know no more than we did before it began. Moi calls for new discussion of what we want from literary criticism today. Is it possible to develop a nonformalist understanding of literary forms?

Rita Felski's chapter has a dual aim: to defend identification and to rethink character. The frequent dismissal of, or disdain for, identification by critics of literature and film arises from several sources. It is often equated with empathy and an excess of feeling—though empathy is just one of several differing means by which readers or viewers identify. It is also confused with identity, with a fixing or circumscribing of the parameters of selfhood. Felski argues that identifying can be ironic as well as sentimental, ethical as well as emotional, may confound a sense of self rather than confirm it, and is practiced by skeptical scholars as well as wide-eyed enthusiasts. It is, in short, a more varied and widespread phenomenon than it is often taken to be.

What readers identify with, above all, are characters. The literary theories of recent decades stressed the status of characters as texts in order to void them of impact or import; imaginary persons, it was argued, were linguistic illusions and bundles of signifiers. By contrast, recent arguments from cognitive and evolutionary psychology minimize the fictionality of character by treating imaginary and real persons as if they were more or less the same. But perhaps it is the fictional qualities of characters that make them real: figures in novels and films are alluring, arresting, alive, not in spite of their aesthetic dimensions, but because of them. That they are fictional does not mean they are stuck fast in the works where they first appear; characters are often translated and adapted, teleporting into new media and milieus. Meanwhile, there are many connections between real and fictional persons: for example, the confusion of character and author in autobiographical fiction; the conflation of character and star when watching a film.

Felski proposes that identifying involves analytically distinct, if often interwoven, strands (alignment, allegiance, empathy, and recognition), drawing on examples from literature and film (*Thelma and Louise*, Thomas Bernhard, Mohsin Hamid's *Exit West*, Camus's *The Stranger*, among others). Her argument that empathy and identification are far from synonymous—that nonempathic identification is not only feasible but common— allows new lines of thinking to open up. Felski introduces the idea of "ironic identification" to clarify how readers become attached to antiheroic protagonists such as Meursault. A sense of estrangement is the connecting tissue binding character and reader: what is held in common is a sense of having nothing in common with others, of feeling disassociated from the mainstream of social life. Patterns of ironic identification also characterize much contemporary scholarship, suggesting parallels between attachments to fictional characters and to charismatic theorists. The chapter underscores the centrality of identification and character to academic as well as lay reading, drawing out similarities between apparently very different modes of response.

Amanda Anderson's chapter explores the importance of character to the literary presentation of moral experience, and in particular to the moral phenomenology of thinking. Anderson proposes that one of the most significant achievements of the novel is its refined capacity to capture interior thought processes, an achievement acknowledged in theorizations and retheorizations of free indirect discourse, stream of consciousness, focalization, and point of view more generally. She is interested in acknowledging and specifying a form of ongoing thought, fundamentally moral in motivation, best captured by the term "rumination." For various reasons, as she shows, the criticism of the past several decades, even including the more recent so-called turn to character, has failed to capture the significance and complexity of rumination as it has been represented in the novel. Partly this has to do with a general tendency to associate character-focused moral criticism with an outmoded and politically problematic humanism. But the larger intellectual inattention to rumination also has to do with certain orienting assumptions of moral philosophy, on the one hand, and cognitive science, on the other, both of which traditions tend to focus on punctual moments of decision and judgment or on publicly visible action and communicable deliberations. Instances of moral decision matter deeply, but so do processes that take place over time, including forms of rumination over experiences of moral shock, status injury, processes of grief and healing, and dawning realizations about the unfolding of consequences.

Literary narratives have a powerful license and capacity to present the interior life, and they do so through complex means, one of which involves the representation of ordinary thought processes, both momentary and sustained. Anderson argues that the English novel since the eighteenth century has been especially noteworthy in capturing forms of rumination, from Richardson (where the epistolary mode externalizes ruminative thought) to Woolf (where stream of consciousness captures the vagaries of attention and the persistence of specific, orienting objects of rumination). Through readings of *Middlemarch*, *The Last Chronicle of Barset*, and *Mrs. Dalloway*, Anderson draws out the complexities of ruminative thinking, noting in particular the tendencies to contrast productive and unproductive forms of rumination. Drawing connections to contemporary cognitive science, moral psychology, and contemporary psychiatric treatments of rumination, this essay defends the centrality of character to our understanding of the distinct contribution of the novel's portrayal of interior moral life. A final section compares the treatment of rumination in Woolf to the discussion of attention and the private moral life in Iris Murdoch's philosophical work *The Sovereignty of Good*.

We want to wrap up these introductory remarks by reaffirming that both writers and readers take a profound interest in characters. Our aim is not to prescribe or prohibit but to open up new avenues of inquiry. To do so, we first need to clear away some old restrictions. Once we understand the origins and nature of the taboo on "treating characters as if they were real," the terrain is wide open. We can, for example, launch inquiries into identification and emotional responses to literature or investigate what characters can tell us about the experience of moral reflection. But our own topics are just examples, not guidelines. We have no wish to lay down requirements for what literary critics must do; we wish rather to encourage explorations of the many different uses of character in literature.

NOTES

We thank Alan Thomas and Randolph Petilos of the University of Chicago Press. Without Alan's vision and Randy's support, this book would not exist. And we are grateful to the anonymous reviewers for helping us to improve our work.

1. Robert Pippin, "Natural and Normative," *Daedalus* (2009): 35–43.

2. Toril Moi, *Revolution of the Ordinary: Literary Studies after Wittgenstein, Austin, and Cavell* (Chicago: University of Chicago Press, 2017); Rita Felski, *Uses of Literature* (Oxford: Blackwell, 2008); Rita Felski, *The Limits of Critique* (Chicago: University of Chicago Press, 2015); Amanda Anderson, *Psyche and Ethos: Moral Life after Psychology*, Clarendon Lectures in English (Oxford: Oxford University Press, 2018); but see also Amanda Anderson, *The Way We Argue Now: A Study in the Cultures of Theory* (Princeton, NJ: Princeton University Press, 2006); Amanda Anderson, *Bleak Liberalism* (Chicago: University of Chicago Press, 2016).

3. Jonathan Culler, *Structuralist Poetics: Structuralism, Linguistics and the Study of Literature* (London: Routledge, 2002), 270.

4. See Roland Barthes, *S/Z: An Essay*, trans. Richard Miller (New York: Farrar, Straus and Giroux, 1974), 191.

5. Culler, *Structuralist Poetics*, 277.

6. Uri Margolin, "Characterisation in Narrative: Some Theoretical Prolegomena," *Neophilologus* 67, no. 1 (1983): 7.

7. See Kendall L. Walton, *Mimesis as Make-Believe: On the Foundations of the Representational Arts* (Cambridge, MA: Harvard University Press, 1993). But note also Richard Moran's telling critique of this book in "The Expression of Feeling in Imagination," *Philosophical Review* 103, no. 1 (January 1994): 75–106.

8. Fotis Jannidis, "Character," in *The Living Handbook of Narratology*, http://www.lhn.uni-hamburg.de/article/character.

9. Alex Woloch, *The One vs. the Many: Minor Characters and the Space of the Protagonist in the Novel* (Princeton, NJ: Princeton University Press, 2003), 15.

10. Ibid., 13.

11. Ibid., 14.

12. John Frow, *Character and Person* (Oxford: Oxford University Press, 2014), 25.

13. Ibid.

14. Ibid., 23.

15. Georg Lukács, *The Theory of the Novel*, trans. Anna Bostock (Cambridge, MA: MIT Press, 1971); Ian Watt, *The Rise of the Novel: Studies in Defoe, Richardson, and Fielding* (Berkeley: University of California Press, 1957); Nancy Armstrong, *Desire and Domestic Fiction: A Political History of the Novel* (New York: Oxford University Press, 1987).

16. Catherine Gallagher, *Nobody's Story: The Vanishing Acts of Women Writers in the Marketplace, 1670–1820* (Berkeley: University of California Press, 1994).

17. Deidre Shauna Lynch, *The Economy of Character: Novels, Market Culture, and the Business of Inner Meaning* (Chicago: University of Chicago Press, 1998).

18. Martha C. Nussbaum, *Love's Knowledge: Essays on Philosophy and Literature* (Oxford: Oxford University Press, 1990).

19. Richard Rorty, *Contingency, Irony, and Solidarity* (Cambridge: Cambridge University Press, 1989).

20. Stanley Cavell, *Disowning Knowledge in Seven Plays of Shake-*

speare (Cambridge: Cambridge University Press, 2003); Stanley Cavell, *In Quest of the Ordinary: Lines of Skepticism and Romanticism* (Chicago: University of Chicago Press, 1988).

21. Robert B. Pippin, *Henry James and Modern Moral Life* (Cambridge: Cambridge University Press, 2000).

22. Murray Smith, *Engaging Characters: Fiction, Emotion, and the Cinema* (Oxford: Oxford University Press, 1995).

23. Marco Caracciolo, *Strange Narrators in Contemporary Fiction: Explorations in Readers' Engagement with Characters* (Lincoln: University of Nebraska Press, 2016).

24. Alan Palmer, *Fictional Minds* (Lincoln: University of Nebraska Press, 2008).

25. Lisa Zunshine, *Why We Read Fiction: Theory of Mind and the Novel* (Columbus: Ohio State University Press, 2010).

26. Blakey Vermeule, *Why Do We Care about Literary Characters?* (Baltimore: Johns Hopkins University Press, 2010).

27. Ien Ang, *Watching "Dallas": Soap Opera and the Melodramatic Imagination* (London: Routledge, 1985); Janice Radway, *Reading the Romance: Women, Patriarchy, and Popular Literature* (Chapel Hill: University of North Carolina Press, 1991).

28. Rachel Sagner Buurma and Laura Heffernan, "The Common Reader and the Archival Classroom: Disciplinary History for the Twenty-First Century," *New Literary History* 43, no. 1 (2012): 11.

29. Frow, *Character and Person*, vi.

30. Derek Attridge, *The Singularity of Literature* (New York: Routledge, 2004), 130.

31. Nora Hämäläinen, "Sophie, Antigone, Elizabeth: Rethinking Ethics by Reading Literature," in *Fictional Characters, Real Problems: The Search for Ethical Content in Literature*, ed. Garry L. Hagberg (Oxford: Oxford University Press, 2016), 18.

32. Ibid., 20–21.

33. Cora Diamond, "The Difficulty of Reality and the Difficulty of Philosophy," in *Philosophy and Animal Life*, by Stanley Cavell, Cora Diamond, John McDowell, Ian Hacking, and Cary Wolfe (New York: Columbia University Press, 2008), 43–90.

34. Hämäläinen, "Sophie, Antigone, Elizabeth," 23.

35. Ibid., 24.

36. For more on Diamond's understanding of attention, and her mode of reading, see Cora Diamond, "Murdoch the Explorer," *Philosophical Topics* 38, no. 1 (2010): 51–85; and also Toril Moi, "The Adventure of Reading: Literature and Philosophy, Cavell and Beauvoir," *Literature and Theology* 25, no. 2 (2011): 125–40.

37. See, for example, the discussion of character in Catherine Gallagher, "The Rise of Fictionality," in *The Novel*, ed. Franco Moretti (Princeton, NJ: Princeton University Press, 2006), 336–63. In her most recent book, Gallagher investigates counterfactual historical fictions and finds that they expand the category of character into the collective and the national. See Catherine Gallagher, *Telling It Like It Wasn't: The Counterfactual Imagination in History and Fiction* (Chicago: University of Chicago Press, 2018).

RETHINKING CHARACTER

Toril Moi

Never treat characters as if they were real people!

INTRODUCING THE QUESTION

Here are some things we can and some things we can't do with fictional characters. And some things they can and can't do with us. We can't libel them. They can't sue us. We can neither murder nor marry them. (So there is no point in warning us against doing any of this.) We can imagine that we talk to them. But they can't talk back. Yet they can place claims on us, claims we may feel compelled to respond to. We can love them, hate them, acknowledge them, imitate them, be inspired by them, carry them in our hearts and minds, think about them when we want to understand our own lives. We can also invent further adventures for them, and we can imagine what they would be like if they lived in our place and time. To understand all this is to understand what fiction is.

When I feel horror, a searing physical discomfort, at watching someone being tortured in a movie (*Reservoir Dogs* or *Pan's Labyrinth* come to mind), my friends sometimes try to comfort me by reminding me that "it's only a movie" (when we say the same thing to children, we don't *remind* them of anything but rather *teach* them, initiate them into our ways of living with fictions)—as if I had forgotten that I was dealing with fiction, as if I took the images to be actual events in the real world. But

I haven't forgotten that I am watching a fiction film. I feel upset because I am watching *a torture scene*. In fact, such reminders can easily become annoying: is the idea that I ought to be able to blunt my sensitivity to torture by focusing on the scene's filmic virtues? Or that my reaction blinds me to the technical points of the scene, so that I can no longer analyze it with the proper critical acumen? But then we are coming close to the idea that emotional responses will always impede critical analysis. And that can't be true. A critic incapable of emotional response will surely miss a lot more than I do.

Academic critics understand this as well as anyone. We are not more likely than others to mistake fictional characters for real people. Yet our discipline is replete with warnings against doing precisely this. Here are some things academic literary critics are told not to do with fictional characters. We must not ask how many children Lady Macbeth had.[1] We must not think of characters as "our friends for life" or say that they "remain as real to us as our familiar friends."[2] We must not talk about the "unconscious feelings of a character," for that would be to fall into the "trap of the realistic fallacy."[3] We must beware of treating "fictional characters as the equivalent of persons [for] it's a tricky business theorizing the ontological hybridity of characters."[4]

Here are some things academic literary critics are urged to bear in mind about fictional characters. We must never forget that "le personnage . . . n'est personne," that the person on the page is nobody.[5] We must always remind ourselves that characters "exist only as words on a printed page" and that "they have no consciousness." Should the "feeling that they are living people" arise, we must firmly repress it, for it is an "illusion."[6] We must remember that if characters fascinate us, it is only because they "invit[e] cathexis with ontological difference."[7] We must also keep firmly in mind that there is always a "tension between thinking of characters as pieces of writing or imaging and thinking of them as person-like entities."[8]

I have wondered for over twenty years—since well before I began working on Henrik Ibsen's modernism—what work these constant reminders and warnings actually do. Unlike Don Quixote, literary critics don't set out to imitate the deeds of their favorite fictional characters. We live in a world in which the concept of fiction has been part of our form of life for centuries. Even little children know that the characters of fairy tales and myths and cartoons don't exist.[9]

I assume that we can agree that no literary critic actually takes fictional characters to be real. But then why do we keep accusing each other of *treating* characters "as if they were real"? What crimes are we trying to prevent? What problems are these constant reminders supposed to solve? What errors are the critics warning us against? Since no academic critic believes that fictional characters *are* real, they are obviously not warning us against trying to kill Othello or marry Mr. Darcy. What exactly is it we must not do? And what would happen if we did it anyway? What is this "treating characters as if they were real"?

To find some answers, I'll look at two exemplary versions of the taboo on taking characters to be real.[10] The first, L. C. Knights's 1933 essay *How Many Children Had Lady Macbeth?*, belongs to the foundational moment of modern academic literary criticism. Although it might be interesting to follow the analysis of Knights's text by a historical tour of the Russian and Czech formalists, the New Critics, structuralism, the theorists of the *nouveau roman*, and the poststructuralists, this would require a book, not a mere essay. Instead, I'll skip straight to the most monumental recent attempt to theorize characters, John Frow's *Character and Person* from 2014.

I'll show that the taboo on treating characters as if they were real originally had far more to do with a specific aesthetic and professional agenda than with philosophical arguments. In 1933, Knights wasn't trying to develop a theory. He was, rather, laying down some ground rules for a serious, professional critical practice. But sometime after World War II, the taboo on treating characters as if they were real people hardened into a dogma. In the 1950s and 1960s, critics of various formalist persuasions began to treat the taboo as a fundamental axiom, that is to say, as a cornerstone for further theoretical and philosophical arguments. The result was theory that silently incorporated Knights's professional and aesthetic agenda—his commitment to professionalizing criticism alongside his commitment to a criticism that could account for modernism—in its foundations. When the taboo on treating characters as if they were real hardened into theoretical *doxa*, it incorporated the aesthetic commitments of modernism. The resulting "modernist-formalist" ethos encouraged literary critics to privilege form over subject matter, prefer "literariness" to "literature," and reject thematic and moral analysis as the expression of naive realism and equally naive humanism. Over time, it became received opinion that any critic who discussed characters "as if they were real people" simply *had* to be a realist humanist or a humanist realist. Theorists began to assume that these despised views were "logically connected" to the idea that one can discuss characters "as if they were real." In this essay I'll show that no such logical necessity exists. What connects the three "forbidden" positions or practices is simply a specific set of aesthetic and professional preferences, which has been mistaken for a philosophical necessity.

There simply is no good philosophical or theoretical reason to accept the taboo on treating fictional characters as if they were real. The real questions raised by this strange taboo are: What should literary criticism be? Does literary criticism have to rest on formalist foundations? How does literary criticism respond to contemporary artistic and intellectual movements? What do literary critics find interesting and important? What kinds of character discussions are we willing to consider sophisticated and intellectually challenging?

A NOTE ON FORMALISM

To avoid misunderstandings, I need to explain what I mean by "formalism." By "formalism" I understand the belief that professional literary critics must privilege form over meaning, themes, or content, often coupled with the belief that there is something unsophisticated, even amateurish about readings that focus on characters, themes, and content. Formalists look for "literariness," cultivate the pleasures of pure textuality, warn their students against the dangers of the "referential illusion," and insist that it makes no sense to ask whether a character "really loves" another character, since they exist only on paper and therefore don't have existential depths.[11] Formalists believe that literary criticism simply *is* the study of form, whether form is understood, as it conventionally has been, as the study of patterns, narrative techniques, figures, and tropes; as an *"arrangement of elements—ordering, patterning, or shaping"*; or as the conviction that "thinking about 'literariness' [is] the special quarry of criticism."[12]

In literary studies today it is common to oppose "formalism" to "historicism," as if we had to choose between doing serious historical (or political) analysis and investigating literary form. I don't think this is an accurate distinction. In my experience, some formalists connect form to politics and history, while others don't. I find it more helpful to distinguish between "pure" formalists, who oppose historical, social, and political analysis, and "political" formalists, who enthusiastically argue for *uniting* formalism and politics.[13]

The second group can be subdivided into "abstract" and "historicizing" political formalists. The "abstract" wing is exemplified in the work of a contemporary critic such as Caroline Levine, who establishes a number of extremely abstract forms that she then offers as instruments for interdisciplinary political analysis. The "historicizing" political formalists came to the fore in the 1980s, when Marxist, feminists, queer, postcolonial, and anti-racist critics began discussing the "politics of form." For them, there was no fundamental conflict between "historicism" and "formalism." Like other formalists, they confidently built on Saussure's understanding of the sign, espoused the modernist aesthetic agenda, and privileged the study of patterns, tropes, figures, and other literary techniques, at the same time as they sought to historicize formal patterns and ascribe ideological meanings and effects to them. (For me, Antony Easthope's 1981 analysis of the ideological effects of iambic pentameter remains an unforgettable example.)[14] "Politics of form" criticism is usually committed to establishing the political and historical significance of a given form. At the same time, it is as obsessed with condensation and displacement, fissures, breaks, cuts, boundaries, and the "beyond" as other kinds of formalism.

I have always felt that my own work has significant affinities to that of the "historicizing" political formalists. But when I studied the reception of Ibsen's plays, I discovered that a monomaniacal search for the "politics of form" can have deeply problematic side effects. Some feminist critics, for example, simply couldn't shake off the belief that realism as a form just *is* intrinsically conservative. As a result they entirely failed to do justice to one of the most radical feminist texts to come out of the nineteenth century, A Doll's House.[15]

Rightly assuming that form can have political effects, such critics wrongly assume that those effects can be established without regard to what the text is about (its "content"). As a result, they take the abstract *form* of realism to trump anything Ibsen or Nora *say*, as if the actual words of the play were of no consequence for its politics. But literary forms simply don't have political essences in isolation from their specific use. And on my Wittgenstein-inspired view, to analyze use is not the same thing as to analyze form and not quite the same thing either as to analyze the contents or themes of a text. It is, rather, to try to understand the text as meaningful form, as form embedded in human practices, as action, expression, and intervention, and as a claim for response.

I am not implying that all contemporary critics are formalists. Nor am I implying that all contemporary critics espouse the taboo on treating characters as if they were real. The manifold varieties of literary criticism simply can't be brought under a single concept in that way. Rather, I think of our discipline as an extensive network of practices and commitments in which some strands overlap and others diverge (see *PI*, §71). I am also well aware that there are critics—including my colleagues in this volume—who have long since set out to break with the modernist-formalist paradigm. But this is no argument against trying to bring out the stakes and commitment of the important strand of literary studies that interests me here: namely, the critical taboo on treating characters as if they were real.

It is time to turn to Lady Macbeth's children. Who is L. C. Knights addressing? Who is he arguing against? What picture of criticism is he promoting? What is at stake for him?

PART I: THE CAMBRIDGE REVOLUTION

HOW MANY CHILDREN HAD LADY MACBETH?

In 1933, when his pamphlet *How Many Children Had Lady Macbeth?* first appeared, L. C. Knights (1906–97) was a twenty-seven-year-old doctoral student at the University of Cambridge. A member of F. R. Leavis's circle, he had just cofounded the legendary journal *Scrutiny*.[16] Knights remained an editor of *Scrutiny* from the first to the last issue (1932–53).

How Many Children Had Lady Macbeth? is a flat-out attack on the belief that it is intellectually interesting to discuss Shakespeare's characters. Pouring scorn on the idea that Shakespeare was first and foremost a "creator of characters," someone uniquely capable of creating men and women as "real as life," Knights singles out A. C. Bradley (1851–1935), the celebrated author of *Shakespearean Tragedy* (1904), as one of the worst offenders (*HMC*, 1). Bradley and other critics of his ilk, Knights argues, show their critical abjection by praising Shakespeare "because he provides 'the illusion of reality,' because he puts 'living people' upon the stage, and because he creates characters who are 'independent of the work in which they appear'" (*HMC*, 26).

Over eighty years after its first publication, Knights's attack on character criticism still makes for fiery reading. Fueled by a revolutionary ambition to transform literary criticism, the essay is a quintessential product of the so-called Cambridge Revolution. Anyone who reads *How Many Children Had Lady Macbeth?* (incidentally, a question not to be found in the essay itself) will notice that the author's intellectual heroes are I. A. Richards and T. S. Eliot, the lodestars of the Cambridge literary avant-garde. Consistently positioning himself as an intellectual on the cutting edge of literary and critical modernism, Knights fights character criticism because he is convinced that it will "condemn *Wuthering Heights, Heart of Darkness, Ulysses, To the Lighthouse* and the bulk of the work of D. H. Lawrence" (*HMC*, 3). Character critics must be stopped in their tracks, for they are incapable of doing justice to the modernist literary canon Knights wishes to promote.

As one might expect from a man of his modernist convictions, Knights rails against realism. Pitting Ibsen against Eliot, he declares that "*Macbeth* has greater affinity with *The Waste Land* than with *The [sic] Doll's House*" (*HMC*, 34). Twice he condemns an obscure tome published in 1923 called *The Old Drama and the New* (*HMC*, 25, 34). Why give it so much attention? The answer is revealing, for this turns out to be William Archer's (1856–1924) last book.[17] Archer, an all-round man of letters, made his name in the 1880s and 1890s by championing Ibsen, translating several of his plays and participating vigorously in the so-called "Ibsen wars" in the British press. In 1933, to condemn William Archer was at once to condemn the late Victorian avant-garde and to recast its members, alongside Ibsen, as a bunch of traditional realists, thoroughly at odds with literary modernism.

Knights's hostility to realism in general (and Ibsen in particular) is typical for the modernist generation. So is his antitheatricality.[18] Anti-realist and anti-Aristotelian, Knights takes theater to be unbearably character and action oriented.

He singles Bradley out for his wrongheaded (Aristotelian) belief that tragedy is "action issuing from character" or "character issuing in action" (*HMC*, 5). Utterly unsympathetic to the idea that tragedy should produce catharsis, Knights also pours scorn on critics who declare that they feel "'quietened,' 'purged' or 'exalted' at the end of *Macbeth* or of any other tragedy" (*HMC*, 54). The intensity of Knights's antitheatricality is such that he even insists that Shakespeare's plays are neither theater nor drama but dramatic *poetry*, or simply *poetry* (see *HMC*, 7, 11, 28, 31, etc.). In fact, the only time the word "revolutionary" occurs in the text is when Knights stresses that critics must turn away from drama and toward poetry: "If we really accept the suggestion, which then becomes revolutionary, that *Macbeth* is a poem," Knights writes, "it is clear that the impulses aroused in Act I, Scenes I and II are part of the whole response, even if they are not all immediately relevant to the fortunes of the protagonist" (*HMC*, 37). At this point, Knights's theory of criticism begins to emerge. Because character critics reduce the play to the fate of the protagonist(s), they miss the crucial thing: namely, the reader's "whole response." But what is this whole response that literary critics should care about instead? And why will we miss it if we are unwilling to think of plays as poems?

Poetry was the genre preferred by I. A. Richards and T. S. Eliot. For them, as for Knights, the critic's task was to bring out the "patterns" of the text. It is entirely possible, even desirable, to produce a brilliant reading of the patterns of a modernist poem without mentioning plot or character; it is much harder to write well about, say, a play by Ibsen without saying a word about these "abstractions," as Knights calls them.

Richards also pioneered the idea of "response" and "total response" crucial to Knights's arguments against character criticism.[19] The task of criticism, Knights writes, is to convey the "total response" (*HMC*, 6), the "total complex emotional response" (*HMC*, 11), the "full complex response" (*HMC*, 24) to the text. "Response," for Knights, as for Richards, is a psychological term describing something that happens in the mind of the reader. The reader's response is an "effect" of the stimulus of the text. The critic's duty, Knights writes, is "to examine first the words of which the play is composed, then the total effect which this combination of words produces in our mind" (*HMC*, 7).

If criticism is to convey the reader's total response to the text, critics must focus on the concrete and the particular, the details of language itself. They must examine the "quality of the verse," the "rhythm and imagery," and "Shakespeare's handling of language" (*HMC*, 17), so as to establish the "pattern" (*HMC*, 50n), the "pattern of the whole" (*HMC*, 64), or the "dramatic pattern" (*HMC*, 28) of Shakespeare's text. In short, they must behave as readers of modernist poetry.

If modernist attention to poetic patterns is concrete, character criticism is abstract: "Wherever we look we find the same reluctance to master the words of the play, the same readiness to abstract a character and treat him (because he is more manageable that way) as a human being" (*HMC*, 26). But this is not all. According to Knights, plot, rhythm, construction, and "all our other critical counters" are abstractions too (*HMC*, 6). But why is he so convinced that "character" and "plot" are abstractions? And why doesn't it occur to him that "pattern," "dramatic pattern," and "total response" are no less abstract? What exactly is abstract about a character in a play? When he tries to justify his claims, Knights's pellucid prose becomes uncharacteristically opaque.

To explain what he means by the "abstraction" of literary characters Knights quotes C. H. Rickword, who had set out to adapt Richards's theories about poetry to the novel. "The form of a novel," Rickword writes (and let's note the emphasis on "form"), "only exists as a balance of response on the part of the reader" (*HMC*, 7). As the reader works through the text, she continuously constructs (and equally continuously revises) the diagram—the schematic outline—we call plot. The same is true for character. Both plot and character are constructed after the fact; they are, therefore, "precipitates from the memory," abstractions which acquire emotional power only "in solution" (*HMC*, 7).[20]

But formulations such as "balance of response" and "precipitates from the memory" are hardly more concrete than "character" and "plot." What exactly are Knights and Rickword trying to say? On closer inspection, the chemical metaphor ("precipitate") turns out to be crucial. A "precipitate" is an insoluble solid that remains once a liquid solution has disappeared. Readers working their way through a text (or audience members seeing a play) experience plot and character "in solution"—as they appear when they are dissolved into the work's full, aromatic mix of flavors and juices. According to this metaphor, to discuss character or plot is like focusing on the desiccated lumps that remain once the original liquid—the experience itself— has evaporated: the result will convey nothing of the reader's actual, living "total response."

Character and plot discussions, then, focus on the "precipitates." Instead of catching the flavor of the work, they only dissect a few specimens preserved in formaldehyde. But criticism should capture the totality of the literary experience in all its freshness. This can be done only by tracking the "patterns" of the actual language of the text. But here the liquid metaphor breaks down. To capture the total response is to capture something like the psychological experience of the work as a whole. But what is the relationship between that experience and the "dramatic pattern" to be mapped out by the impersonal, antisentimental modernist critic? Maybe we are to imagine it as something akin to spectral-wave analysis—a detailed registration of the frequency, depth, and amplitude of waves in a liquid. But if so, the resulting graph tells us nothing about the *experience* of traversing the storm-tossed ocean.

Knights's arguments in favor of tracking patterns and conjuring up the total response are unconvincing in two different ways. First, the appeal to Richards's theory of total response feels strained. It makes his argument murky. Second, as we have just seen, the contrast between abstract and concrete which is supposed to ground the rejection of character criticism simply doesn't work. Leaving total-response talk aside, the rest of his argument—the idea that we have to choose between the wish to study the "unique arrangement of words that constitutes" the play (HMC, 32) and the wish to discuss characters and plot—survives to this day.

COUNTERARGUMENTS

Knights pits character analysis against attention to the "words themselves." Theoretically or logically, this opposition makes little sense. After all, characters and plot are made up by the same unique arrangements of words that Knights wishes to investigate. Moreover, he provides no reason to believe that we somehow can't understand (can't capture the "full response" to) a text which contains characters unless we avoid any discussion of those very characters. I am hardly the first to point this out. In 1969, Stanley Cavell noted that the taboo on character talk appeared to be grounded on no real arguments: "[The critic] has been made to believe or assume, by some philosophy or other, that characters are not people, that what can be known about people cannot be known about characters, and in particular that psychology is either not appropriate to the study of these fictional beings or that psychology is the province of psychologists and not to be ventured from the armchairs of literary studies. But is any of this more than the merest assumption; unexamined principles which are part of current academic fashion?"[21]

Fifty years later, Cavell's diagnosis of the taboo—"merest assumption; unexamined principles"—remains uncannily relevant. But today the skepticism signaled by Cavell has been reversed, for now there is a widespread conviction that what *can* be known about characters *can't* be known about people.[22] While the talk in the 1960s may have been about "psychology," today we are more likely to hear about the "unconscious" or "affects." Yet Cavell's point remains valid: most of the claims advanced as reasons for not taking an interest in literary characters come across as so many unmoored bits of philosophy. The taboo turns out to be a veritable iceberg of unexamined theoretical assumptions.

This is certainly true for the idea that critics must "shift" from character criticism to "verbal analysis"—criticism taking an interest in "general patterns of meaning, systems of image or metaphor or symbol" (AL, 267). While not denying that such talk captures something important in the history of literary criticism, Cavell thinks that the significance of the shift is not well expressed by setting up an opposition between characters and words, since we never really choose between them: "How could any serious critic ever have forgotten that to care about a specific character is to care about the utterly specific words he says when and as he says them; or that we care about the utterly specific words of a play because certain men and women are having to give voice to them?" (AL, 269).

In any case, there is more than one way to pay close attention to the words on the page. One way, Cavell writes, is to focus on ambiguities, patterns, tensions, so as to bring out the "(more or less hidden) structure of which the individual words are parts" (AL, 268). Another is to pay attention to *voice*, to the "phenomenology of the straits of mind in which only those words said in that order will suffice" (AL, 269). The former is the way of New Criticism or, in a different mode, of the hermeneutics of suspicion; the latter is that of ordinary-language philosophy.

"The most curious feature of the shift and conflict between character criticism and verbal analysis," Cavell declares, "is that it should have taken place at all" (AL, 268). I agree. There is no fundamental conflict between paying attention to language and paying attention to characters. Good critics of characters do both. Others have seen this too. In the 1970s, for example, Seymour Chatman showed that A. C. Bradley's much-maligned character analysis in *Shakespearean Tragedy* is in fact grounded in detailed scrutiny of Shakespeare's language.[23]

So why have generations of literary critics found the idea of a conflict and a shift so convincing? The obvious reason is that such talk actually captures a genuine difference in critical *practice*. What could be more striking than the difference between an essay discussing characters' motivations and intentions, their emotions, moral dilemmas, and existential crises, and an essay focusing on language, structures, and patterns? Clearly, an essay on imagery in *Macbeth* will be utterly different from an essay dissecting the characters' moral dilemmas. But this is a difference grounded in the critic's aesthetic, intellectual, and professional preferences and interests, not in some kind of inexorable logical necessity. There is no fundamental reason why a critic can't mix character analysis and formal analysis, or why she can't enrich her moral character analysis with convincing analysis of verbal patterns. To understand why Knights's arguments won the day, we need to understand what his professional and aesthetic preferences were and how his essay promoted them.

THE MOMENT OF MODERNISM: KNIGHTS'S PROFESSIONAL AND AESTHETIC AGENDA

I have already shown that Knights promotes modernist aesthetics by signaling his hostility to nineteenth-century realism and to drama and theater. I have also shown that this project is profoundly inspired by I. A. Richards and T. S. Eliot. Now I want to take a closer look at his cultural and professional references. Who does he attack? Who does he defend? I'll show that Knights had a clear aesthetic and professional agenda: promoting a new, professional literary criticism and enthroning the modernist aesthetics of the late 1920s and early 1930s as the new touchstone for critical practice. His ambition, in short, was to ensure that professional literary criticism would be a practice capable of doing justice to modernism, his time's most innovative, and most controversial, aesthetic movement.

Knights's main targets are gentlemen scholars, professional writers, women, and cultural products tainted by middlebrow taste and popular success. In his classic book on the *Scrutiny* movement, Francis Mulhern notes that the circle around *Scrutiny* saw themselves as the "vanguard of the 'highbrow' front in culture."[24] Knights's highbrow modernist taste is obvious. He dislikes realist writers (Ibsen, Hugh Walpole, John Galsworthy) and their admirers (William Archer). He expends much energy denouncing the famous actress Ellen Terry's [*Four*] *Lectures on Shakespeare*.[25] As if to excuse the overkill, he notes—signaling his antipopular stance as he goes—that "Ellen Terry of course does not represent critical Authority; the point is not that she could write as she did, but that the book was popular" (*HMC*, 4). In the same way, he dismisses one of Terry's contemporaries in the theater, the manager-actor Herbert Beerbohm Tree, and pours scorn on two nineteenth-century women writers whose immensely popular books on Shakespeare's heroines had remained in print for almost a century: Anna Jameson's *Shakespeare's Heroines: Characteristics of Women, Moral, Poetical, and Historical* (1832) and Mary Cowden Clarke's *The Girlhood of Shakespeare's Heroines* (1850).

Almost all Knights's targets had their heyday before World War I. As we have seen, he is particularly keen to distance himself from the previous avant-garde: the late Victorian and Edwardian realists, for whom Ibsen represented the last word in daring aesthetic innovation. But he also detests the Romantics. Most of Knights's *bêtes noires* are artists (writers, actors, theater directors), and quite a few are (dead) women. All these targets have one thing in common: they are critical *amateurs*.

On the whole, Knights steers clear of criticizing professional academics. This is not wholly surprising, since there still wasn't much of a professional tradition to attack. English had only recently been established as a university discipline in Britain. A. C. Bradley had held a chair at Glasgow and was Professor of Poetry at Oxford for five years, but in 1932 he was long since retired. Logan Pearsall Smith, who specialized in editing anthologies of

English writers, lived off the income of his American family's business.[26] Knights does not mention the holder of the King Edward VII Chair at his own university, the well-connected gentleman scholar Sir Arthur Quiller-Couch. On the other hand, he promotes the latest professional criticism, singling out for praise two women academics, both of whom had just earned their PhDs and published their first book: Q. D. (Queenie) Leavis (1906–81) and Muriel Bradbrook (1909–93).[27]

As a highbrow modernist, Knights heaps scorn on the popular and the middlebrow, blaming the rot of character criticism on the "growth of the popular novel, from Sir Walter Scott and Charlotte Brontë to our own Best Sellers, [which] encouraged an emotional identification of the reader with hero or heroine" (HMC, 25). Such "Best Sellers" make a "direct appeal to human sympathy and emotion," which "can only vitiate Shakespeare criticism" (HMC, 23). Because character criticism applies "moral and realistic canons" to Shakespeare's plays, it's responsible for the unbearable "sentimentalizing of his heroes," Knights writes (HMC, 27).

Good criticism, on the other hand, requires a certain kind of impersonality, what Knights calls the critic's "necessary aloofness from a work of art" (HMC, 28). I read this as a reference to T. S. Eliot's well-known theory of the poet's aesthetic impersonality: the critic is to be as impersonal as the modernist poet. (As we have seen, Knights also embraces I. A. Richards's idea that the critic is to grasp the "total emotional response" to a work. For this not to be contradictory, Knights would have to distinguish between something like a disciplined emotional response and mere sentimentality.)

Knights's references also express a sociological and cultural position. Mulhern notes that the members of this group were mostly middle or lower-middle class. Embracing I. A. Richards's critique of the "bellettristic subjectivism" that dominated criticism until after World War I, the new Cambridge critics saw themselves not as amateurs and gentlemen but as professionals.

They felt no affinity for the "leisurely and expansive connois-seurism" associated with Quiller-Couch and many other pre–World War I critics. They "prized analytic and judicial rigour," Mulhern writes, but also "drew freely on the resources of other disciplines and laid strong emphasis on the reciprocal relations between literature and its social and cultural context."[28]

Knights's critical agenda is now clear. Against traditionalist, feminized, middlebrow sentimentality he sets cool, modernist impersonality. Identification, emotional responses, sympathy, and moralism must go, for they serve only to cloud the critic's gaze. Since thinking of texts as creating the "illusion of reality" (*HMC*, 4) encourages these vices, it's not just character criticism but realism itself that must go. These are not coherent philo-sophical arguments but expressions of the avant-garde aes-thetic agenda of Knights's generation. In the 1920s and 1930s, traditionalist critics attacked modernist artists and writers precisely by arguing that they were immoral, incapable of in-venting emotionally satisfying plots, and failed to provide characters with which one could sympathize. (In the 1880s and 1890s similar accusations were levied against Ibsen.) No wonder Knights attacks precisely such forms of critical response.

I admire Knights's campaign on behalf of modernism. I think he does what all ambitious young critics set out to do: find a way to do criticism—to do their life's work—that promotes the kind of literature they care about. I also think that literary criti-cism always participates in—and contributes to—the cultural, intellectual, and aesthetic movements of its day. Of course we should write criticism that expresses our own aesthetic prefer-ences and our own political and philosophical interests. In fact, I believe that—apart from hypocrisy—we have no other option: this is what we do.

But if I admire Knights's stance, what, then, is the prob-lem? To see that, we must distinguish between Knights's use of certain arguments and the use of the same arguments by later critics. My analysis places Knights firmly in his own time and place. Given his specific intellectual and professional situation, Knights's project makes sense. Knights is also utterly clear on what his agenda is and what he wants to achieve. That his actual arguments aren't always convincing is true. However, it doesn't follow that the opposition he faced at the time had better ones. I am sure that if I had been a young academic critic in the United Kingdom in the early 1930s, I too would have revolted against the staid old gentlemen critics waxing sentimentally about the "humanity" of Shakespeare's heroes.

But what happens when the same arguments (we must focus on verbal patterns, not on characters; we must not treat characters as if they were real people) get used by different critics writing in new and different situations? Uttered under new and different circumstances, what looks like the same theoretical claim may not in fact *be* quite the same claim. (This is surely why Wittgenstein thought of giving *Philosophical Investigations* the epigraph "I'll teach you differences.") In the history of literary criticism, postwar movements—New Criticism, Russian and Czech formalism, structuralism, poststructuralism—embraced some of the same positions as Knights, but often to quite different effects.

Three points must be made about the different postwar uptakes of the character taboo. (1) They share Knights's promodernist agenda, including his anti-realism and antitheatricality. (2) They accentuate the incipient formalism of the Cambridge Revolution far more than Knights does, for the members of the *Scrutiny* group weren't formalists in the sense that they opposed historical and cultural analysis. On the contrary, they were deeply engaged with the effort to understand language and literature as a vital part of social community. (Knights's own first book was full of social and historical analysis of Shakespeare's England.) Yet Knights's emphasis on "patterns" and on the "words themselves" lent itself very well to more militantly formalist positions. (3) The postwar movements developed a taste for theory absent in Knights's (very British) essay. Whereas

Knights (on the whole) argues for a specific critical *practice*, postwar critics of various formalist persuasions set out to build *theories*, often in the belief that every practice must be grounded in a theory. But a theory is a different beast from a simple practical recommendation, for now critics begin to talk about logical necessity, theoretical principles that must be respected, and so on (I return to this in part II, below).

But if Knights's arguments aren't all that convincing, why did they nevertheless win the day? Knights's essay did not cause the postwar assault on character criticism. Although it remained in print until well into the 1970s, it was never central to the theory generation. While the New Critics had some knowledge of *Scrutiny*, the Russian and Czech formalists created their own tradition well before *Scrutiny* was founded. I also doubt that the members of the various postwar French theory movements read Knights. Rather, his essay stands as a radical new beginning precisely because he responded to the cultural and professional situation of his day and because that situation turned out to be exemplary of that of later generations of critics. Whether they were European or North American, the postwar generation of critics admired modernism and sought to develop a kind of criticism that could do justice to its best writers. After the war, that meant not just Proust and Joyce but Celan and Beckett too.

In any case, arguments don't always carry the day. New critical and aesthetic agendas are usually promoted and adopted not because they are philosophically more convincing than older ones but rather because they respond better to new aesthetic (or intellectual or political) concerns. Here we touch on questions that animate much of Wittgenstein's later thought: Are we always swayed exclusively by reasons? How much work can explanations do? If critics change their minds about fundamental issues in their discipline, do they do it more as a result of a "conversion experience" than as a result of a cool, dispassionate examination of reasons? Why do some arguments seem so decisive at a certain moment, only to lose their power a generation later? None of this implies that literary critics are more irrational than other academics, for Thomas Kuhn asks the same kind of questions about scientists in his brilliant (and Wittgenstein-inspired) book *The Structure of Scientific Revolutions*.[29]

In my view, the taboo on character talk became truly problematic only when it congealed into a new critical *doxa*, an unchallenged, taken-for-granted dogmatic claim that was no longer subjected to critical examination. When the taboo on treating characters as if they were real hardened into theoretical dogma, that dogma incorporated the pro-modernism and accentuated the formalist agenda already present in Knights's essay. But while Knights promoted his specific aesthetic agenda openly and self-consciously, later critics have not always been aware of the modernist-formalist bias built into their own theories. When they go on to apply the new theoretical *doxa* to all kinds of literature, the result can be breathtakingly anachronistic, as when postwar critics impose their modernist-formalist categories on Ibsen's plays and then complain that Ibsen naively represents reality, clings to overly theatrical paradigms, and generally lacks aesthetic self-consciousness.

Once Knights's passionate promotion of a new, modernist-inflected, highbrow, professional criticism had been pried loose from its historical and cultural moment and turned into a simple theoretical dogma ("don't ever treat characters as if they were real people"), critics would refuse to acknowledge interesting work that failed to fit with their *parti pris*; would blind themselves to obvious facts (become unable to see, for example, that both Bradley and Cavell pay scrupulous attention to Shakespeare's words). Eventually, some would set out to build vast new theoretical structures on nonexistent foundations.[30]

How Many Children Had Lady Macbeth? exudes the energy of a young man who knows he is fighting the good fight against a moribund, amateurish, upper-class critical establishment. Knights's attack on character criticism is a call to arms on behalf of a new, professional, academic literary criticism, a passionate intervention in the struggle to establish a future for a new generation of critics for whom the aesthetics of modernism was a self-evident touchstone. As such, it was immensely successful. The future that Knights hoped for in his youthful essay did in fact come to pass. Postwar critics did become professional academics who took for granted that criticism should take place within a modernist-formalist framework. And once that system was in place, a critic who appeared to treat characters as if they were real would quickly realize that this was not the way to earn symbolic capital in a profession built on the belief that such procedures are naive and simplistic. Thus, criticism explicitly drawing on identification, emotional responses, and moral or ethical discussion of characters and their behavior came to be perceived as the sign of amateurs at work.

PART II: THE TABOO AS THEORY

JOHN FROW: THE ONTOLOGY OF FICTIONAL CHARACTERS

The professional ideals promoted by the Cambridge Revolution still police the boundaries of our discipline. We don't want our students behaving like fans, or like Knights's despised lady writers gushing over Shakespeare's heroines. And when interlopers from other disciplines dare to discuss literature, we shut them out as soon as they fail to show the required interest in form. This is why so many critics (including myself) can't find much to admire in the way most moral philosophers treat literary works. So much discussion of the moral dilemmas of different characters and so little attention to genre, style, and form!

For Knights, as we have seen, the taboo on taking characters to be real was largely a recommendation of a certain critical practice. But sometime after World War II, critics became dissatisfied with mere practice. They required theory. Much of the crucial theory formation in the period from the 1960s to the early 1990s was explicitly formalist. In this period the already-strong formalism of literary studies was powerfully reinforced by the post-Saussurean vision of language, which considers the sign itself to be split: the signified is pure concept; the (material) signifier, pure form. The result was a far-reaching privileging of theories based on ideas about the "materiality of the signifier" (or the "mark"). Any such theory will by definition be formalist.[31] Literary studies today, then, are dominated by a two-headed troll: formalism and theory. Both draw on and incorporate the pro-modernist agenda that inspired the first generation of professional academic critics. In the 1960s, the aim of a group such as *Tel Quel*, for example, was not just to produce a theory that could do justice to the most avant-garde forms of modernism but to produce a theory that would itself be modernist. In addition, the formalist theory formations in themselves inspire an increasingly formalist interpretation of modernism, to the point that after a while it began to be difficult to recover the first modernists' own understanding of what they were doing.

I won't dwell on the history of criticism. Instead, I'll leap straight to the new millennium, for around 2000, things began to change. The heyday of the linguistic turn was over, and the formalist straitjacket had begun to chafe. Critics began to want to discuss characters in literature without feeling that they were committing a theoretical *faux pas*.[32] In 2003, Alex Woloch's brilliant exploration of minor characters in the nineteenth-century novel, *The One vs. the Many*, made a pioneering attempt to open the way for a freer relationship to characters and character criticism.[33]

Woloch begins by reminding us of Aristotle's distinction between a narrative focusing on one hero (poetry) and one focusing on many characters (history). How do different kinds of narratives handle the "surge of many people into a single story"? How do "living persons get rendered into literary form"?[34] These imaginative questions inspire Woloch to develop an account of how "character-space" and "character-systems" shape minor characters in the works of Jane Austen, Charles Dickens, and Honoré de Balzac. While Woloch remains fundamentally concerned with the structure and shape of spaces and systems, he also succeeds in making formal analysis more receptive of ordinary ways of thinking about character. While this was not necessarily a revolution in critical thinking about character, it *was* serious reform.

The most ambitious attempt to produce a full-scale theory of literary characters, John Frow's *Character and Person*, was published in 2014. An immensely learned and wide-ranging book, *Character and Person* covers every imaginable aspect of character theory in literary studies. While the towering ambition and the wealth of examples make for a certain sprawling digressiveness and a knotted density of style, Frow's key points are clear enough.

First of all, Frow is a self-declared formalist: "'Character' is a concept of form. . . . I work within a formalist tradition" (*CP*, x). His impressive range of examples, one reviewer notes, "favors literary innovation . . . and modernist experimentation."[35] Inheriting the modernist-formalist understanding of character ushered in by Knights, Frow sets out to refine and improve it. But, unlike Knights, Frow ranges far beyond mere literary concerns: his goal is to explore both "how [fictional] characters work as quasi-persons" and "how social personhood works as a kind of fiction" (*CP*, vii). Frow sets out to bring together formalism and social analysis, or, in his own words, to contribute to a "sociological poetics concerned with the social force of representation" (*CP*, x). The goal is to create a literary theory capable of overcoming what he takes to be the opposition between formalism and historicism.

In the following, I will focus on Frow's key arguments about characters and leave his claims about persons aside. To try to keep the argument as clear as possible, I'll do this in four steps. (1) I'll first look at Frow's fundamental picture of characters. (2) Then I'll turn to his suggestions for how to talk—and not to talk—about characters. (3) I'll pause to point out the striking parallels between Frow's understanding of characters and the post-Saussurean tradition's understanding of the sign. (4) Finally, I'll explain why I think Frow's way of setting up the problem of characters as well as his conviction that we need to talk about characters as "ontological hybrids" are attempts to solve a nonexisting problem. In the course of the argument it will become clear that my disagreement with Frow is not just a disagreement about how to think about literary character but a more fundamental clash between Frow's conventional mode of doing theory and my own Wittgensteinian understanding of what theory is and what work it can do. I will show that "character talk" is best understood as a language-game in Wittgenstein's sense of the term (as expressed in *PI*, §23). But if this is right, then no further theorizing is possible.

1. What Characters Are: Frow's Project

Frow's starting point is the perfectly ordinary observation that fictional characters—"these clusters of words or images" (*CP*, 1)—move us. For Frow, there is something miraculous about this. He is overcome by wonder. This is understandable enough. Both Plato and Descartes thought that wonder was the very hallmark and origin of philosophy. But, as Wittgenstein reminds us, wonder can also be misplaced and misleading. He gives the example of a philosopher who has become transfixed by the problem of names and tries to grasp the nature of naming—the essential connection between a thing and its name—by "staring at an object in front of him and repeating a name or even the word 'this' innumerable times" (*PI*, §38). In such cases, we have what looks like a philosophical problem but in fact is empty language (language "on holiday"; *PI*, §38). Instead of looking at how we use names, the philosopher has fallen prey to the idea that naming must be an "occult process" that stands in need of a theory (*PI*, §38). I will show that something similar is going on with Frow's wonder at characters.

But first we need to understand Frow's reasoning. Looking at the clusters of words, Frow wonders how it can be that those clusters move us, make us respond to them. How can dead signs have such effects on us? Frow's answer is that characters must be extremely "complex conceptual entit[ies]," which stand in need of a clarifying theory (*CP*, 25). He begins by proposing that characters are "ontologically hybrid beings" (*CP*, 1). By this he means that characters are at once "pieces of writing or imaging" and "person-like entities" (*CP*, 2, 25). This creates a self-evident tension that must be resolved: "I seek to resolve that tension by proposing that fictional characters must—in ways that I think are logically difficult to hold together—be seen to be both at once" (*CP*, 2).

Frow repeatedly insists on the *logical* difficulty of holding together the fact that characters are at once "pieces of writing" and "person-like entities," and wonders how it can be that we do this so effortlessly in everyday life: "[T]hese two ways of thinking about character are logically difficult to hold together; and yet we do so in our every encounter with fictional character: the problem is to find a language in which to convey this ontological hybridity" (*CP*, 25). I doubt that there is a *logical* problem here (I'll return to this), but I note Frow's call for a new (theoretical) language in which to talk about characters.

Here is my best overview of Frow's project. He begins by noticing that we naturally and effortlessly respond to fictional characters with emotions, affects, identification, and moral and political judgment. This is our (public and shared) way of dealing with fictional characters. To Frow, this practice is at once remarkable and puzzling. His wonder arises from the fact that he takes as axiomatic that "character" is split into two parts: words or images here, "person-like entities" there. This is the "hybridity" of characters. How can it be that we so effortlessly hold these two parts together in everyday life? This ordinary feat stands in need of "logical" explanation. (Theory is required.) Ordinary ways of talking blind us to the problem, for we talk as if characters were real people. But this obscures the hybridity of characters. We therefore need a language capable of conveying—reminding us of—their hybridity at all times. In practice, this seems to mean that we need constantly to remind ourselves that characters are textual entities. This would explain why Frow is so hard on critics who, like Woloch, occasionally lapse into more ordinary ways of talking about characters.

2. Character Talk

Frow's project, then, is to find a new language in which to talk about characters, one which draws attention to their essential hybridity. His *bête noire* is character talk that in *any* way, however implicitly, suggests that characters live on outside the texts they appear in.[36] It is certainly not enough for critics simply to declare that they know perfectly well that characters aren't real human beings. Thus, critics who have tried to figure out the identity of the narrator in Vladimir Nabokov's notoriously complex novel *Pale Fire* get smacked on the knuckles for the "inherent absurdity" of their readings, which reveal that they are unable to treat characters as "textually based effects" (*CP*, 31).

This seems too harsh. It is difficult to believe that critics working on the intricate narrative structures of Nabokov's novel would be in danger of overlooking the fact that they are dealing with textual creatures. Yet, according to Frow, as soon as they speculate about characters or invent fanciful stories to explain who the narrator of the text is, they fall into the trap of treating characters as if they were real. They fail to realize that the character called Kinbote "is made of words," that "his reality is an effect of the modality of the textual world to which he belongs, and of the intermodal play between the novel's worlds" (*CP*, 32). Apparently, then, any discussion of characters' intentions and motivations must be outlawed, for such speculations will of necessity imply that the characters do or think something when they're off stage or off page. There is no place in Frow's theoretical universe for such ordinary ways of talking about characters.[37] How, then, should we talk about them?

To understand Frow's recommendations for character talk, we need to look more closely at his analysis of the two aspects of fictional characters. He begins by asking the ontological question "What kind of things are literary characters?" (*CP*, vi). He then provides two traditional answers and declares that he wishes to overcome the split they imply. The first is the "ethical answer": "characters are to be treated and analyzed as though they were persons, having lives that transcend the texts they appear in." The second is the "structuralist answer" (personally, I would call this the "formalist answer"): "characters are to be treated purely as textual constructs" (*CP*, vi).

Strikingly, both answers are prescriptions, not definitions. Neither the ethical nor the structuralist answer says anything about what characters are. The formalist answer comes closest, for it implies that characters are textual constructs. But the ethical answer *doesn't* say that characters are real people. On Frow's own account, "ethical" critics treat characters "*as though* they were persons" (my emphasis). But we usually don't say that we treat an entity *as though it were* something if it *is* that something. (I wouldn't usually say that I treat my fork *as though* it were a fork; see *PI*, pt. 2, §122.) Even Frow himself acknowledges that ethical critics don't in fact believe that characters *are* persons any more than the structuralist critics do. This is why I am not convinced that these answers provide two competing "ontologies" of character. (If all parties think that characters arise in words, where is the ontological difference?)

Frow fudges the issue by declaring that the ethical answer "tends to conflate textually formed entities with persons" (*CP*, vi). But "tends to conflate" introduces a philosophical wobbliness that makes it hard to follow the argument. (Do they or don't they? And what are we to take that "conflate" to mean exactly?) In any case, Frow doesn't say that the ethical critics treat characters "as though they were real people"; rather, he says that they

treat them "as though they were *persons*." So now everything
hinges on what a "person" is. To bring that out, I'll simply list
five key claims in Frow's analysis:

- A "person" is a "slightly more abstract and structural way of
  talking about people" (*CP*, v).
- Character is "both . . . a formal construct, made out of words or
  images and having a fully textual existence, and . . . a set of effects
  which are modelled on the form of the human person" (*CP*, vi).
- "Fictional character is a person-shaped figure made salient by
  narrative ground" (*CP*, 24).
- There is a "tension . . . between thinking of characters as pieces of
  writing or imaging, and thinking of them as person-like entities"
  (*CP*, 25; but see also *CP*, 2).
- Characters are "ontologically hybrid beings" (*CP*, 1; see also
  CP, 25).

When Frow writes that a character is a "person-shaped figure" or a "set of effects . . . modelled on the form of the human
person," this doesn't mean that characters represent or refer to
real people. Nor does it mean that characters are shaped like
persons. It means that they are shaped like the *form* of persons,
as long as we bear in mind that a "person" is not in fact a person but a "slightly more abstract and structural way of talking
about people." To make sure that we keep these thoughts firmly
in mind, Frow frequently refers to characters as "quasi-persons"
(*CP*, vii) and "person-like entities" (*CP*, 25).

But the murky terrain of "entities" and "quasi-persons" is
confusing. In the end, I am not at all sure what the ethical critics
are accused of doing wrong. Frow is working too hard to set up
an "ontological" or "conceptual" opposition for a phenomenon
we would be better off discussing under the heading "disagree-
ments about critical practice." How should we discuss characters? What kinds of character talk are we willing to acknowledge
as excellent literary criticism? Frow doesn't really advance that

debate. In practice, he defaults to one of the more formalist versions of the old taboo: remember always to remind yourself and your readers that characters are textual entities.

3. Is the Sign Dead?

I am struck by the parallels between Frow's account of characters and the post-Saussurean account of the sign. I don't mean to argue that Frow consciously bases his argument on that account, for he never says that he does. I just mean that the logic of the argument is exactly the same. Frow begins by positing that characters are split in two. They are mere clusters of words, mere text. Yet in our minds they live. They are, then, at once pieces of writing and the mental or psychological response they produce in us.

I completely agree that this is what characters are: pieces of writing (or filmmaking) that come alive in our minds. (That's what I try to convey right at the beginning of this essay.) The problem is not the conclusion (or should that be the starting point?). The problem is the idea that we will reach this insight only if we begin by positing a split between words and meaning and then invent a theory to explain how they come together.

Frow's understanding of characters exactly mirrors the post-Saussurean understanding of the split sign. The signifier is taken to be pure form without meaning, pure materiality, nothing but black marks on a page. The signified is the concept, the event in our minds which gives meaning to the signifier. (This is one version of what Wittgenstein calls the "Augustinian picture of meaning"—theories that posit a split between word [pure materiality or sound] and meaning [a concept in our minds or, alternatively, a thing in the world].) This view invites us to ask what holds the two parts together and to try to provide a theory—an explanation—to bridge the gap.

This view of language splits meaning from form, form from meaning. While critics carry out this operation after the fact, they go on to present it as a starting point or foundation. In this way they quickly forget that in language, meaning and form are always intertwined. This point is so important to me that I'll briefly spell out some of the reasoning that leads me to say this.

Critics, like everyone else, spontaneously understand linguistic signs and sounds (in languages they understand) as "meaningful forms." As Saussure acknowledges, meaning is fundamental to even the most formal linguistic operations. Every time we split a sequence of sounds or letters into linguistic units, we do so on the basis of their meaning. We say that English distinguishes between the phonemes /k/ and /m/ because we already know that the meaning of "cat" is different from the meaning of "mat." If we didn't know this, we wouldn't know where to begin.[38] For specific purposes (say, a wish to study phoneme systems or the transformations of Indo-European consonant systems over time), such formalizing operations are just fine.

The trouble begins only when the split sign is taken to be the *foundation* for the "meaningful form" we actually hear or read. For now the critic, or the theorist, appears to have forgotten that she herself began by understanding the utterance as a meaningful form. It is as if the critic first helps herself to the meaning, then pretends that she is faced with nothing but an empty form (the "mark," the "empty signifier"). Insofar as studies of form in literary studies build on versions of this (split) picture of the relationship between form and meaning, they will be formalist in the sense I use the word. It is formalist in the extreme, for example, to define characters exclusively as "clusters of words" or to consider a text to be nothing but a "set of signifiers."

Taken out of context, dragged out of their living use, signs do seem lifeless. When we look at a word or phrase in isolation, for example, we can be struck by the distance between the dead sign and the living meaning. "Every sign *by itself* seems dead," Wittgenstein observes. "*What* gives it life?—In use it *lives*. Is it there that it has living breath within it?—Or is the *use* its breath?" (*PI*,

§432). In *use* the deadness of the sign (its propensity to come across as empty form) disappears.

Writing well after the linguistic turn has ceased to seem as compelling as it once did, Frow doesn't speculate about the connection between the signifier and the signified. Instead, he turns to the more fashionable concept of ontology. But now we can see that to claim that *characters* are "ontological hybrids" is exactly like claiming that the Saussurean *sign* is an "ontological hybrid." "Ontologically" the signifier is a material form. As for the signified or the "concept," it is difficult to say what its ontology actually is. Philosophers tend to settle for one of two options: either the concept is an "abstract object" or it is a "mental representation." (Saussure explicitly defined the signified as the latter.) Given that the Saussurean sign unites the material and the conceptual, we can of course call it an ontological hybrid as well. But then all we are saying is what we already knew: that characters are made up of words (or images) and have the power to appeal to us, move us, place claims on us. Only a formalist vision of language—one in which we begin by understanding the words themselves as empty or dead—can invent a problem here. In ordinary life, characters pose no questions to which "ontological hybrid" is the answer.

In my view, the question of what holds signifier and signified together is a pseudoproblem, one that arises from the theorists' own picture of meaning. There is no point in inventing yet another theory for how to connect signifier and signified, for it is the assumption of a fundamental split that is the problem. The same is true for characters. The term "ontological hybrids" does no work. We end up knowing what we already know: that we often respond powerfully to literary characters and often discuss them in terms we also use about real people. In the same way, only someone who has fully accepted the taboo on treating characters as if they were real will believe that a phrase like "quasi-persons of narrative" (*CP*, 23) does more work than the word we already have: namely, "characters."

4. Ontology and Logic: A Different View

I am, in short, unconvinced by Frow's picture of how characters work. I think he becomes spellbound by the idea that there *must* be something wondrously complicated going on, something deep and mysterious, something that only the most magnificent theoretical effort can grasp. Or in other words: I think Frow forgets how to "look and see," forgets to remind himself of our ordinary and everyday practices with characters.

Wittgenstein writes about a similar problem, one that arises when philosophers discuss why it is that propositions have meaning. In the following quotations, I have replaced "proposition" by "character" to highlight the point: "One person might say, 'A [character] is the most ordinary thing in the world,' and another, 'A [character]—that's something very remarkable!'— And the latter is unable simply to look and see how [characters] work. For the forms of the expressions we use in talking about [characters] and thought stand in his way" (*PI*, §93). According to Wittgenstein, the forms of our expressions and the importance we attach to the subject are precisely the features that risk seducing us into "thinking that something extraordinary, even unique, must be achieved by [characters].—A *misunderstanding* makes it look to us as if a [character] *did* something strange" (*PI*, §93).

The theorist of character, then, is in danger of overlooking the plain and ordinary ways we deal with characters: "For our forms of expression, which send us in pursuit of chimeras, prevent us in all sorts of ways from seeing that nothing extraordinary is involved" (*PI*, §94). "Nothing extraordinary is involved." To understand what characters are, we need to look at how we talk about them. If we do, we will discover that we seem to have no fundamental intellectual problem in dealing with them. The philosopher Ted Cohen puts it plainly: "Ordinary readers, and extraordinary ones as well, do commonly say they are having real feelings about fictions, and they name these feelings with the same words they use when naming feelings they have about real, existent things."[39] Yet nobody has any problem understanding what ordinary speakers mean when they talk about characters in such ways.[40] In particular, nobody accuses them of not understanding that characters aren't actually living human beings. We could say: This is how this particular language-game is played. We often talk about fictive characters in much the same way we talk about real people, and yet we don't get confused, don't begin to mistake fiction for reality. (Here one could launch a discussion of what fiction is, but that is clearly a different question.)

If theorists wish to turn ordinary ways of talking about characters into a problem, they need to do more than declare that there simply *must* be a problem, that it simply *must* be impossible to have "real feelings about things known not to exist."[41] For that is, after all, what people consistently say they have, without confusing either themselves or others. And feelings are just one example. People also feel kinship and identification with characters. They feel that characters place claims on them, as if they were asking for a response. Such experiences are among the reasons we read fiction (and nonfiction), and it makes no sense at all to exclude them from consideration.

Frow insists that characters present us with a *logical* problem: the problem of how we hold the textual signs together with the emotional responses. I don't think this is a logical problem at all. Cora Diamond's remark that, in philosophy, terms like "logically possible" or "conceptually possible" often "indicate some kind of confusion" springs to mind.[42] To respond to fictional characters with emotions (and so on) is just what we do. To ask for a logical explanation of this practice is like asking for a logical reason why water at sea level boils at 100 degrees Celsius. Or like asking for a logical reason why a sentence means what it means in a given situation.

Wittgenstein writes: "Our mistake is to look for an explanation where we ought to regard the facts as 'proto-phenomena.'

That is, where we ought to say: *this is the language-game that is being played"* (*PI*, §654). By "proto-phenomena" Wittgenstein means something like bedrock, a phenomenon that doesn't call for further justification and explanation. A language-game isn't a philosophical problem. It's just what we do and say. What could count as a philosophical explanation of "inviting" or "ordering"? "The point is," Wittgenstein continues, "not to explain a language-game by means of our experiences, but to take account of a language-game" (*PI*, §655). Among his examples of language-games Wittgenstein mentions "acting in a play" and "making up a story, and reading one" (*PI*, §23). In my view, there's every reason to consider "talking and writing about fictional characters" as a language-game in its own right, on a par with others (praying, begging, asking, questioning, for example). But if this is right, then we have reached the end of our inquiry.

I don't want to stop anyone from asking what a fictional character is. I just want to indicate that the answer will be found, not in speculation, but in an examination of use—that is, in how we talk about characters. For how do we establish the "ontology" of something? According to Wittgenstein, "Grammar tells what kind of object anything is" (*PI*, §373). He means that if we want to know what something is, we should undertake a grammatical investigation, which means looking at how we talk about that something. Because use is systematic, public, and shared, we can create a map, an outline, of the "grammar" of the relevant words, expressions, language-games. In this exercise, world and words are intertwined. The result will be, not an overarching definition, but descriptions, a series of examples (see *PI*, §71) that will enable us to see the phenomenon in question more clearly.

To give an example: In *The World Viewed*, which has the subtitle *Reflections on the Ontology of Film*, Stanley Cavell asks what film is.[43] But readers searching for a single, overarching definition of film will be disappointed. Cavell doesn't set out to define an "ideal cinematic essence"; rather, he seeks to provide what

Burke Hilsabeck calls an "open-ended and phenomenological" account of film.[44] He is mapping the *grammar* of the phenomenon, refusing to lay down requirements for what "film" must mean in advance of any particular example of its use. Instead, he sets out to describe and analyze what we do with—how we use and respond to—various aspects of film. In the same way, I would argue, we understand what characters are by looking at how we talk about them, how we use and respond to them, and not by trying to subsume them under a more or less metaphysical concept ("ontological hybrids," for example).

If we begin by splitting the textual aspect of characters from our ordinary responses to them, we will most likely conclude that we now need a theory to connect the textual entity to the response. But if we found such a theory, it would bring us right back to where we started, to the point where ordinary readers (including those ordinary readers who also happen to be literary critics) *begin*: with the fact that we do respond in myriad ways to characters as they appear onstage or on the page. So what is the explanatory power of the idea that we must constantly be aware of the ontological hybridity of characters? In practice, it all seems to boil down to an immense effort to impose a kind of formalist language police on literary criticism. The glory of *Character and Person* is Frow's acknowledgment that we need to be able to talk about emotions and identification, about motivations and intentions, and about the claims characters place on readers. But Frow's formalism traps him, and he can't get out.

WHAT NOW?

I have shown that the taboo on treating characters as if they were real is intertwined with the promotion of a specific understanding of modernist aesthetics and with the belief that formalist analysis is the *raison d'être* of professional literary criticism. I have also shown that the taboo rests on no sound philosophical grounds, and that there is no need to roll out a whole theoretical machinery in order to authorize ourselves to talk about characters in ordinary ways.

The question now is what the implications of these claims are. If I tear down the taboo, am I obliged to replace it with a new theory of characters? Or at least to supply a blueprint for future modes of reading? And what about the modernist-formalist paradigm? Am I against any attempt to consider literary form? What is the difference between formalist and nonformalist ways of thinking about form?

Before I continue I may have to stress the obvious: I am not arguing that characters *are* real people. (It's over four hundred years since Cervantes first made fun of that idea.) Nor am I arguing that we should *only* say about characters things we would also say about real people, for ordinary character talk is clearly not limited in that way. When I complain that some novel has an insipid heroine or an implausible hero, for example, I am mobilizing aesthetic criteria of judgment which usually would make little sense in relation to my friends. (If I were to use such terms about my friends, it would probably be in an attempt to be witty or crack a joke.)

I am not arguing, either, that no situation could ever arise in which a literary critic might find a good reason to tell another critic that she should remember that characters are textual creatures. But such a reminder would arise in response to a specific problem and would precisely not have the status of a general taboo. In this essay, I fully acknowledge this by stressing that, in Britain in the 1930s, L. C. Knights had excellent reasons for waging war against the belletristic character analysis of the older generation of gentlemen critics. Problems arise only when we turn the response to a specific problem or situation into unquestioned *doxa*.

Underlying the automatic rejection of character criticism is the modernist-formalist assumption that such criticism always presupposes a naive realism, a giving in to the "referential illusion," and a commitment to an antediluvian humanism. But ordinary character talk is as varied as ordinary language itself. Ordinary language doesn't prevent us from disagreeing about anything. If we jettison the taboo, we would still quarrel about subjectivity and humanism. We just wouldn't make the mistake of assuming that character talk *per se* promotes one view of these matters rather than another.

There is also the assumption, already quite evident in Knights's essay, that formal analysis is always difficult and intellectually demanding, whereas character analysis is always easy and unchallenging. Thus, the former requires professionals, while the latter can be left to amateurs. This goes along with the idea that character talk will always be empty-headed, overemotional, moralizing, sentimental gushing. Such assumptions are false. But they are still with us. If I am right, then the question is not whether character criticism should exist but how to create intellectually sophisticated character criticism.

But what about practical criticism, the so-called tension between considering characters as textual phenomena and as fictional human beings? There is after all an obvious difference between arguing that the end of *Jane Eyre* expresses Jane's love for Rochester and arguing that it expresses the requirements of a certain Victorian narrative structure.[45] I have tried to show that these are not *logical* opposites but examples of different critical *practices*, which arise in response to different questions. If I want to know about love in Victorian literature, I will have to do different kinds of research, focus on different aspects of a text, than if I am interested in Victorian narrative structures. But there is no logical or theoretical conflict between these two lines of inquiry. And there is certainly no need to imply that one is always intellectually superior to the other.

It is true that as things stand today, the formal reading will sound more sophisticated to most literary critics' ears. But that is because critics have spent almost a hundred years promoting formalism. Most of us are simply better at teaching students how to analyze narrative structures than how to think about love. Yet "love" has a long, deep, and complex history in philosophy and theology, a history containing ideas that are no less challenging than theories of narrative structure.[46]

In any case, I am not arguing that we must forget everything we have learned about literary forms. I am arguing that we make a mistake when we forget that literature is not *just* form, forget that it is made up of world-bound language that always conjures up themes, ideas, images, situations—contents—too. In my experience, it is perfectly possible to combine humanly interesting discussions of characters with formal analysis. In many cases, the former reinforces and enhances the latter. To a large extent, Ibsen expresses his awareness of the problems of theater and theatricality through his characters. His characters theatricalize themselves, or others, and live to suffer the consequences. Critics who refuse to engage with his characters will simply not discover the extent of Ibsen's metatheatrical awareness. Paradoxically, their own modernist-formalist bias blinds them to Ibsen's pioneering modernism.

A good reading begins when the critic notices something and asks, "Why this?"[47] The way we deal with characters (or form or history) will depend on what we want to find out. Different questions will require different procedures, different kinds of research, different kinds of answers. But such differences are not evidence that there is a theoretically (or "logically") problematic tension inherent in the concept of character itself. They are just evidence that there are many different kinds of critical practice. Each critic will have to discover her own questions, stake herself—her own experience and judgment—in her criticism, show us what she sees, and take responsibility for her own choices.

*
**

Some readers of earlier versions of this essay have felt that it ends just when the real work ought to begin. Surely, they said, the purpose of writing such a long analysis of the taboo on treating characters as if they were real people can only be to clear the ground for a new theory of character. That surprised me. For I take myself to have shown that "talking or writing about characters" is a language-game in its own right. And, as Wittgenstein stresses over and over again, language-games—practices in which world and word are intertwined—are not grounded on any theory or philosophy. One can't *explain* a language-game, if by that one means finding a foundational reason for why it is as it is. A language-game is simply what we do and say. Were I now to turn around and propose a theory purporting to ground or explain the language-game I call "talking or writing about characters," I would be contradicting myself rather badly, as if I had failed to understand the implications of my own analysis.

This conclusion may seem disappointing. Wittgenstein was well aware that his way of doing philosophy often appeared to lead to nothing grand: "Where does this investigation get its importance from, given that it seems only to destroy everything interesting: that is, all that is great and important? (As it were, all the buildings, leaving behind only bits of stone and rubble.) But what we are destroying are only houses of cards [*Luftgebäude*] and we are clearing up the ground of language on which they stood" (*PI*, §118). Like Wittgenstein, I think there is genuine value in showing that what we take to be deep insights are in fact critical or philosophical illusions.

I take this essay to be an analysis of the historical and cultural conditions of possibility for Knights's views on character criticism and of the philosophical "picture" that governs Frow's assumptions about characters. Once we realize that the picture in question is not compulsory, it no longer holds us captive. Call that an analysis of the theoretical conditions of possibility for his theory of character. Historical and cultural analyses, and philosophical investigations of this kind, aren't preludes to further work. They *are* the work.

But my readers may have other ideas about what a "theory" is. Perhaps they want me to set forth my own ideas for how to read characters, as if there could ever be only *one* way of doing that. In any case, I don't believe in laying down requirements for what good character analysis must look like in advance of any specific practice. The time for investigation is *after*, not *before*, the utterance. Or perhaps my early readers wanted me to provide a model reading, one that could inspire future readings of characters. I have written a number of recent essays in which I analyze characters.[48] But those essays aren't attempts to *apply* anything. They are, rather, attempts to *respond* to features of a text that have grabbed my attention.

But, my readers might say, you could at least tell us what kind of work you *would* do were you to work more systematically on character in literature. Well, I could certainly imagine investigating character in a novel, an author's *oeuvre*, a genre, or a period. But I would do so only in response to a genuine question I might have about the material. I imagine the result would be something like a map of that specific region of the vast field of literary characters. The map would be offered as an attempt to find my way, to see something clearly. It would be not a "theory" but rather a "surveyable representation" or a "clear view," what Wittgenstein calls an *übersichtliche Darstellung* (PI, §122). And while such work might benefit from this essay (for at least I wouldn't be held back by the old taboo, and I would also be on guard against the temptation to project modernist-formalist categories on to my material), it still would require a fresh investigation of new terrain.

*
**

Finally, a word about leaving the modernist-formalist paradigm behind. Modern academic literary criticism arose and was consolidated alongside, and as part of, the canonization of modernism. It is not surprising that our discipline imported a number of beliefs associated with the way critics from the 1930s through the 1960s understood modernism. Knights is just one salient example. But if we fail to be aware of this, we will project those historically specific ideals and beliefs on to writing produced under quite different conditions. This has, to a large extent, been the case in Ibsen criticism, for example. I hope this essay will spur more debate about this problem.

Like Knights, I too have an aesthetic agenda. I have always been drawn to writers working before, alongside, or in the margins of the high modernist revolution, such as Ibsen and Simone de Beauvoir. More recently, I find myself fascinated by certain kinds of new writing, the kinds that put the difference between fiction and reality under pressure, in which authors are characters, and characters are declared to be real. This writing sometimes calls itself fiction and sometimes nonfiction. It sometimes comes with the label "memoir" and sometimes with the label "novel." How relevant is the taboo on taking literary characters to be real for a critic wishing to understand Karl Ove Knausgård's *My Struggle* or Sheila Heti's *How Should a Person Be?*

To deal with such texts, we need to move beyond the modernist-formalist paradigm. We need to develop nonformalist analyses of form. By "nonformalist" I mean analyses of form that don't take modernist notions of what form is for granted, analyses that realize that literary forms always come embedded in world-building language that conveys specific meanings, themes, and subject matter, analyses that realize that texts are never just forms but also expressions, actions, and interventions. Such a starting point would widen our understanding of what a formal analysis is and inspire interest in features of literary texts often overlooked by formalists.

Description is one such feature. The modernist-formalist paradigm tends to reduce description to mere "reference," a sign of old-fashioned realism. But as I explain elsewhere, in the case of Knausgård's *My Struggle* concepts such as "reference" or the "reality effect" don't really help us to understand what is going on.[49] In this case, terms such as "*expression*" and "*attention*" are far more illuminating. Knausgård's descriptions reveal what he sees, what he pays attention to, and express his yearning for reality. They express his powers of imagination and invite us to judge the quality of his attention. They build the world of *My Struggle*. To assess and analyze description, we may, as the memoirist Patricia Hampl suggests, need to reach for terms such as "style," "voice," and "integrity."[50] Above all: description conjures up a world for the reader. A text is not a set of signifiers (or marks or signs or "textual entities" or forms) in search of a meaning. A literary text gives us a world. The task of literary criticism is not to reduce that world to pure form but to account for it in its full complexity, including its forms.

I began with a simple question about the taboo on treating characters as if they were real. But now I find myself thinking about the end of a paradigm. The question, then, is not about character. The question is whether we want formalism and its underlying allegiance to a particular version of modernist aesthetics to remain the defining essence of our profession. The question, in short, is exactly what L. C. Knights took it to be when he first raised the question of character criticism: What should academic literary criticism be?

NOTES

I am grateful to Hannah Haejin Kim for her comments on an early version of this essay, and to Niklas Forsberg for inviting me to present a different version at the conference "Ethics: Form and Content" organized by the Centre for Ethics: A Study in Human Value at the University of Pardubice in the Czech Republic in May 2018. As so often, my essay has benefited from the insight of my friends and colleagues Christine Hamm and Sarah Beckwith. Rita Felski's and Amanda Anderson's questions and comments vastly improved my work.

1. L. C. Knights, *How Many Children Had Lady Macbeth? An Essay in the Theory and Practice of Shakespeare Criticism* (1933; New York: Haskell House, 1973). Hereafter references to this work will be abbreviated *HMC* and page numbers given parenthetically in the text.

2. Hugh Walpole, *The Waverly Pageant* (1932), quoted in *HMC*, 2; Logan Pearsall Smith, "On Reading Shakespeare" (1932), quoted in *HMC*, 5.

3. Mieke Bal, *Guidelines for Writing a PhD Thesis within ASCA* (Amsterdam: ASCA [Amsterdam School for Cultural Analysis], 2006), 30.

4. From a 2017 reader's report on the proposal for this essay.

5. Charles Grivel, *Production de l'intérêt romanesque* (1973), quoted in Catherine Gallagher, "The Rise of Fictionality," in *The Novel*, ed. Franco Moretti (Princeton, NJ: Princeton University Press, 2006), 350.

6. O. B. Hardison Jr., *Aristotle's Poetics* (1968), quoted in Seymour Benjamin Chatman, *Story and Discourse: Narrative Structure in Fiction and Film* (Ithaca, NY: Cornell University Press, 1978), 117.

7. Gallagher, "Rise of Fictionality," 357.

8. John Frow, *Character and Person* (Oxford: Oxford University Press, 2014), 2. Hereafter references to this work will be abbreviated *CP* and page numbers given parenthetically in the text.

9. A number of philosophers have investigated the nature of fiction. In general, their discussions don't appear to have consequences for the practices of literary critics. In "Rise of Fictionality," Gallagher elegantly summarizes some relevant debates. Two key texts are John R. Searle, "The Logical Status of Fictional Discourse," in *Expression and Meaning: Studies in the Theory of Speech Acts* (Cambridge: Cambridge University Press, 1979), 58–75; and Kendall L. Walton, *Mimesis as Make-Believe: On the Foundations of the Representational Arts* (Cambridge, MA: Harvard University Press, 1993). I found Richard Moran's thoughtful critique of Walton's foundational assumptions illuminating. See Richard Moran, "The Expression of Feeling in Imagination," *Philosophical Review* 103, no. 1 (January 1994): 75–106.

10. I mean "exemplary" in the sense of cases that are good to think with, examples that bring out significant features of the phenomenon under analysis. I am also thinking of Wittgenstein's discussion of examples in *Philosophical Investigations*, §71. See Ludwig Wittgenstein, *Philosophical Investigations: The German Text, with an*

English Translation, trans. G. E. M. Anscombe, P. M. S. Hacker, and Joachim Schulte (Malden, MA: Wiley-Blackwell, 2009). Hereafter references to this work will be abbreviated *PI* and section numbers given parenthetically in the text. For a discussion of the implications of §71 for theory building in the humanities, see chapters 3 and 4 in Toril Moi, *Revolution of the Ordinary: Literary Studies after Wittgenstein, Austin, and Cavell* (Chicago: University of Chicago Press, 2017). Instead of peppering this essay with references to *Revolution of the Ordinary*, I will just say that anyone interested in the background and foundations for my claims about language and theory in this essay can find them in *Revolution of the Ordinary*.

11. The example comes from Hélène Merlin-Kajman's fascinating account of the clash between the "professional" reading habits of professors of literature and the same professors' "private" reading habits: *Lire dans la gueule du loup: Essai sur une zone à défendre, la littérature* (Paris: Gallimard, 2016), 23.

12. The first quotation comes from Caroline Levine, *Forms: Whole, Rhythm, Hierarchy, Network* (Princeton, NJ: Princeton University Press, 2015), 3 (emphasis in the original); the second from Jonathan Kramnick and Anahid Nersessian, "Form and Explanation," *Critical Inquiry* 43, no. 3 (2017): 667.

13. Kramnic and Nersessian's "Form and Explanation" exemplifies "pure" formalism; while Frow's *Character and Person* and Levine's *Forms* both strike me as versions of "political" formalism.

14. Antony Easthope, "Problematizing the Pentameter," *New Literary History* 12, no. 3 (1981): 475–92.

15. In chapter 1 in Toril Moi, *Henrik Ibsen and the Birth of Modernism: Art, Theater, Philosophy* (Oxford: Oxford University Press, 2006), I give a detailed account of why various kinds of historicist criticisms—which I there call "culturalism"—usually turn out to be various kinds of politicized formalism (see esp. 17–36). This current essay brings together the views on language, theory, and criticism in *Revolution of the Ordinary* and my views on modernism, realism, formalism, and theater, as well as my critical practice in *Henrik Ibsen and the Birth of Modernism*. Had I not worked on Ibsen, including

his reception in Britain, I would surely not have recognized the aesthetic agenda of L. C. Knights's references so readily, for example.

16. Knights founded *Scrutiny* in 1932, in collaboration with the American Donald Culver and under the close supervision of F. R. Leavis. Leavis himself took on editorial responsibility only after the first two issues turned out to be a roaring success. See Francis Mulhern, *The Moment of "Scrutiny"* (London: New Left Books, 1979), 41. See also Christopher Hillier, *English as a Vocation: The "Scrutiny" Movement* (Oxford: Oxford University Press, 2011), 229.

17. William Archer, *The Old Drama and the New: An Essay in Re-valuation* (1923; New York: Dodd, Mead, 1929). Knights omits the author's name.

18. For more on antitheatricality and modernism, see my own book on Ibsen, *Henrik Ibsen and the Birth of Modernism*, as well as Michael Fried's classic *Absorption and Theatricality: Painting and Beholder in the Age of Diderot* (Chicago: University of Chicago Press, 1980). For a history of antitheatrical attitudes, see Jonas Barish, *The Antitheatrical Prejudice* (Berkeley: University of California Press, 1981).

19. These terms were first coined by I. A. Richards. It is no coincidence that Knights's exemplary reading of *Macbeth* begins with a reference to Richards's 1929 book *Practical Criticism* (see *HMC*, 31). For more on Richards's influence on modern literary criticism, see Pamela McCallum, *Literature and Method: Towards a Critique of I. A. Richards, T. S. Eliot and F. R. Leavis* (Dublin: Gill and MacMillan Humanities Press, 1983); and Joseph North, *Literary Criticism: A Concise Political History* (Cambridge, MA: Harvard University Press, 2017).

20. Knights takes these quotations from C. H. Rickword, "A Note on Fiction," published in *The Calendar*, October 1926. *The Calendar*, which lasted for only two years, was *Scrutiny*'s precursor. Later, Knights repeats the formulation "precipitates from the memory" in his own voice (see *HMC*, 31).

21. Stanley Cavell, "The Avoidance of Love: A Reading of *King Lear*," in *Must We Mean What We Say?* (Cambridge: Cambridge Uni-

versity Press, 2002), 268. Hereafter references to this work will be abbreviated AL and page numbers given parenthetically in the text.

22. Gallagher ("Rise of Fictionality," 356) writes: "Narratorial omniscience, indirect discourse about the mental states of characters, and representations of interior monologues, for example, all portray the 'intimate subjective experiences of . . . characters, the here and now of their lives to which no real observer could ever accede in real life.'" Gallagher is quoting Dorrit Cohn, *The Distinction of Fiction* (Baltimore: Johns Hopkins University Press, 1999), 24.

23. See Chatman, *Story and Discourse*, 134–38.

24. Mulhern, *Moment of "Scrutiny,"* 34. Mulhern adds that he found the expression "'highbrow' front" in a "four-page publicity brochure issued by the editors [of *Scrutiny*]" in 1934 (see 34n87).

25. Ellen Terry (1847–1928) wrote her lectures at the beginning of the twentieth century and then toured extensively performing them. The manuscripts were published posthumously in 1932. For interesting reflections on Terry's lectures as texts intended for performance, see Lynne Truss, "Rereading Four Lectures on Shakespeare by Ellen Terry," *Guardian*, July 27, 2012, https://www .theguardian.com/books/2012/jul/27/four-shakespeare-lectures -ellen-terry.

26. In 1950 Edmund Wilson penned a withering takedown of Smith's literary pretentions, in "Virginial [sic] Woolf and Logan Pearsall Smith," *New Yorker*, May 27, 1950, 99–105, https://www .newyorker.com/magazine/1950/05/27/virginial-woolf-and-logan -pearsall-smith.

27. See Q. D. Leavis, *Fiction and the Reading Public*, originally a dissertation written under the supervision of I. A. Richards (1932); and Muriel Bradbrook, *Elizabethan Stage Conditions* (1932).

28. All quotations in this paragraph are from Mulhern, *Moment of "Scrutiny,"* 25.

29. Thomas S. Kuhn, *The Structure of Scientific Revolutions* (Chicago: University of Chicago Press, 1970).

30. This development was further promoted by the midcentury theory wave: the post-Saussurean vision of language, the so-called

critique of the subject, and the increasing prestige of "theory" itself, which I can't go into here.

31. For an excellent critique of the "mark," see Walter Benn Michaels, *The Shape of the Signifier* (Princeton, NJ: Princeton University Press, 2004).

32. In the first decade of the new century, journals also set out to reconsider character. In 2006 the annual *Shakespeare Studies* published a special "Forum," edited and introduced by Rafael Falco, called "Is There Character after Theory?," with contributions from Alan Sinfield, Jonathan Crewe, Dympna Callaghan, Christy Desmet, Elizabeth Fowler, and Tom Bishop (*Shakespeare Studies* 34 [2006]: 21–74). In 2011 *New Literary History* devoted a special issue to character, with an introduction by Rita Felski and contributions from Amanda Anderson, Sara Ahmed, Julian Murphet, Murray Smith, Suzanne Keen, Catherine Gallagher, and Paisley Livingston and Andrea Sauchelli (*New Literary History* 42, no. 2 [Spring 2011]: v–ix, 209–360).

33. Alex Woloch, *The One vs. the Many: Minor Characters and the Space of the Protagonist in the Novel* (Princeton, NJ: Princeton University Press, 2003).

34. Ibid., 11.

35. Julie Orlemanski, review of *Character and Person*, by John Frow, *Modern Philology* 115, no. 4 (December 2017): E000, doi:10.1086/695968.

36. This is Knights's point too, but Frow doesn't refer to *How Many Children Had Lady Macbeth?*

37. As Seymour Chatman (*Story and Discourse*, 117) pointed out a generation ago, such unnatural restrictions will make for uninteresting criticism: "Should we restrain what seems a God-given right to infer and even to speculate about characters if we like? Any such restraint strikes me as an impoverishment of aesthetic experience. Implication and inference belong to the interpretation of character as they do to that of plot, theme, and other narrative elements."

38. The last three sentences are taken from Moi, *Revolution of the Ordinary*, 116–17.

39. Ted Cohen, *Thinking of Others: On the Talent for Metaphor* (Princeton, NJ: Princeton University Press, 2009), 36.

40. See *ibid.*, 37. Gallagher, who writes in a very different spirit, also notes that however often we are warned against having emotions about fictional characters, we still do. See Gallagher, "Rise of Fictionality," 352.

41. Cohen, *Thinking of Others*, 36.

42. Cora Diamond, "Rules: Looking in the Right Place," in *Wittgenstein: Attention to Particulars; Essays in Honour of Rush Rhees (1905–89)*, ed. D. Z. Phillips and Peter Winch (New York: St. Martin's Press, 1989), 20.

43. Stanley Cavell, *The World Viewed: Reflections on the Ontology of Film* (Cambridge, MA: Harvard University Press, 1979).

44. Burke Hilsabeck, "The 'Is' in What Is Cinema? On André Bazin and Stanley Cavell," *Cinema Journal* 55, no. 2 (2016): 26, 25. In general, Hilsabeck provides an interesting discussion of Bazin's and Cavell's different—or not so different—ways of answering "ontological" questions.

45. I am grateful to Rita Felski for the example.

46. For just one example of philosophical attempts to analyze love in relation to fiction and film, see Susan Wolf and Christopher Grau, eds., *Understanding Love: Philosophy, Film, and Fiction* (New York: Oxford University Press, 2014).

47. I discuss the implications of the "Why this?" question in chapters 8 and 9 of *Revolution of the Ordinary*.

48. I try to develop nonformalist ways of talking about characters in two recent essays on *Hedda Gabler*. See Toril Moi, "Hedda's Silences: Beauty and Despair in *Hedda Gabler*," *Modern Drama* 56, no. 4 (2013): 434–56; and Toril Moi, "Hedda's Words: The Work of Language in *Hedda Gabler*," in *Ibsen's "Hedda Gabler": Philosophical Perspectives*, ed. Kristin Gjesdahl (New York: Oxford University Press, 2018), 152–73. A third essay, "Acknowledging the Other: Reading, Writing, and Living in *The Mandarins*," is forthcoming in *Yale French Studies* (2019).

49. In a recent online essay on Karl Ove Knausgård, I begin to

develop a nonformalist account of description as a literary form. See Toril Moi, "Describing *My Struggle*," *The Point*, December 27, 2017, https://thepointmag.com/2017/criticism/describing-my -struggle-knausgaard.

50. See Patricia Hampl, "The Dark Art of Description," *Iowa Review* 38, no. 1 (2008): 77.

IDENTIFYING WITH CHARACTERS

Rita Felski

Many of us have felt a tug of connection with a character in a novel or a film: a sense of affinity or shared response. We explain this tie by saying we are *identifying*. But how, exactly, are we drawn in? What kinds of ties are being forged? There is often a carelessness when critics talk about identification: the experience is judged before it is fully seen. It is often held to be slightly shameful—something that other people do (the naive, the unschooled, the sentimental). Yet identifying is a default rather than an option; a feature, not a bug. Two forms of confusion have led critics astray. Identification is often equated with *empathy*, or co-feeling—though empathy is just one of the ways in which readers and viewers identify. And it is also conflated with the question of *identity*, with a fixing or circumscribing of the parameters of selfhood.

Both assumptions are ripe for reassessment. Audiences become attached to fiction in an abundance of ways; these ties can be ironic as well as sentimental, ethical as well as emotional. Identifying involves ideas and values as well as persons; may confound or remake a sense of self rather than confirming it; and is practiced by skeptical scholars as well as wide-eyed enthusiasts. In short, it is more varied and more pervasive than it is taken to be. Tackling the academic disdain for identification as a naive or "bad" reading practice, Faye Halpern points out that "sophisticated literary critics read to identify as well. The difference comes not from the practice of identification but from the differing *grounds* of identification."[1] What, then, are these differing grounds? What are the beliefs, hopes, habits, or obsessions that lead readers or viewers to identify in specific ways? What part is played by a text and what kind of intermediaries are involved? Why audiences care about fictional figures, how they treat them as matters of concern—such questions deserve closer scrutiny.

To rethink identification is also to rethink character. We can think of characters as being like persons without scanting or shortchanging their aesthetic qualities. Neither do we need "the illusion of reality" to identify—an assumption that fails to account for attachments to Bugs Bunny, Cinderella, or Vladimir and Estragon. Characters do not have to be deep, well-rounded, psychologically complex, or unified to count as characters; nor, of course, do they need to be human. They need only to be *animated*: to act and react, to will and intend.[2] Why do critics so often equate character with the genre of realism—whether they come to bury or to praise it? Audiences identify with figures from fairy tales, comic strips, melodramas, parables, and superhero movies, not to mention *Star Trek*, *The Texas Chain Saw Massacre*, or *Blood and Guts in High School*. The draw of character has far less to do with realism than with qualities of vividness and distinctiveness. As any cartoonist knows, a few well-chosen strokes can be far more effective than a detailed rendering; stylization is a powerful tool. In "Notes on 'Camp,'" for example, Susan Sontag writes: "character is understood as a state of continual incandescence—a person being one very intense thing."[3] Identification is as relevant to *Malone Dies* as to *Middlemarch*, to *Tom and Jerry* as to *Doctor Zhivago*—though the *mechanisms* of identification will certainly vary.

The messiness of how we identify runs up against two intellectual temptations: overpoliticizing and overpsychologizing. At a certain moment in film studies, the first tendency ran rampant; a gamut of aesthetic experiences was boiled down into a single story line. Mixing up cocktails of Freud, Marx, and Mulvey, critics excoriated any form of identification as a trap: a means by which viewers were seduced into complicity with the status quo. Identification had to be "broken down" in order to make critical thinking possible. (The intensity of their own identifications with critical theory and theorists, meanwhile, went entirely unremarked.) The recent turn to cognitive psychology has led to much more fine-grained accounts of the mental processes that bind us to works of art. And yet the connections to a larger world and agencies beyond the self are often lost. Reading these accounts, one gets the impression that identifying is a drama being played out in the cloistered cells of individual minds.[4]

I've learned a great deal, nonetheless, from cognitive-oriented film critics such as Murray Smith and Carl Plantinga. They both point out—with some justification—that "identifying" is a slippery and confusing word, and they opt instead to speak of "engaging." Yet this strikes me as a case where the cure is worse than the disease. Engagement covers an even broader and more diffuse range of reactions: being turned on by, disgusted by, or falling in love with characters, for example, as well as identifying with them. My own interest lies squarely with identification as used in everyday speech: to describe an affinity that is based on some sense of similarity. This commonsense usage, as we'll see, does not exclude complexity; to be like a character is not synonymous with *liking* a character: a felt affinity can be underwritten by diverse, conflicting, or ambivalent affects. Meanwhile, these shared qualities may motivate or inspire identification (as when we are drawn to a work of fiction that captures something already known); or they may be produced *by* identification (as when we temporarily "take on" or assume aspects of fictional figures). By contrast, when a group of British women interviewed by Jackie Stacey reflected on their love of moviegoing in the 1940s, some of them stressed the utter remoteness and unattainable glamor of an actress such as Rita Hayworth; she was "out of this world," someone to be worshiped from afar. "I adored Ava Gardner's dark magnetism," commented one interviewee, "but knew I wasn't like that."[5] Here devotion is tied to the frisson of difference: to a perceived chasm between viewer and Hollywood star. There is an intense engagement, but it has very little to do with perceived similarity and identification.

Identifying, then, implies a sense of something shared, but this does not mean obliterating or overriding differences. There is no Vulcan mindmeld, no fusion of viewer and character where we lose all sense of self or capacity for independent thought.[6] To identify with something is not to be identical with it; we are talking about the rough ground of resemblance rather than pure sameness. There is a rich vein in cultural studies—especially its feminist variant—that is devoted to the complexities of how audiences identify; that this work is so rarely acknowledged in literary theory, film theory, and philosophical aesthetics is unfortunate. My argument builds on these ideas rather than recapitulating them, but I want to underscore my debt to the groundbreaking work of Ien Ang, Jackie Stacey, Janice Radway, Judith Mayne, and others.[7]

The existence of queer studies, meanwhile, pivots on the possibility of identifying across identities (Douglas Crimp), on a view of identifications as mobile, elastic, and volatile (Diana Fuss).[8] And here aesthetic identifications—to characters, stars, authors—are selective, speaking to an affinity with certain qualities rather than with the whole person: "I never wanted to be her," writes Jim Elledge of Tina Turner; "I just wanted her strength, her self-assuredness and a body I wasn't ashamed of." They can be empathic, involving a shared sense of pain or abjection: Christopher Murray ponders the phenomenon of gay attachment to "tragic figures of ridicule" such as Margaret Dumont, the comic foil of the Marx Brothers movies. They can be a matter of comeuppance: Edward Field writes of larger-than-life movie stars who represent "yearnings for vindication, in which we see ourselves transcending the difficulties a gay man faces in the world." They can be as much about style as about selfhood: "it's in the shape of my sentences and the trajectory my thinking follows that I find her lambent voice and habits of mind limning my own" (Brian Teare on Virginia Woolf).[9]

And here identifying does not simply entrench a prior self but may enrich, expand, or amend it. Perhaps we glimpse aspects of ourselves in a character, but in a way that causes us to revise our sense of who we are. The phrase "shock of recognition" is not just a cliché. We can be sustained, but also disconcerted, by a felt kinship with a fictional figure. Estrangement is not the opposite of identification but its shadow; it is not uncommon to sense the alien or unappealing aspects of a character one is being drawn to.[10] And while something shared is key, the nature of this "something" cannot be predicted ahead of time. Is it temperament or social situation; feelings, histories, or values; who one is or who one would like to be? That audiences can identify with a hobbit or a rabbit is a sign that semblances are often metaphorical rather than literal. Affinities experienced while reading a book or watching a film can cut across divisions of gender, race, sexuality, class, or even, in certain genres, species. It is a matter not just of finding oneself but of leaving oneself. In her autobiography, Jeanette Winterson speaks of "reading herself" in the mode of fiction as well as fact, as the only way of keeping her story open. She is transported into alternate worlds, even as these worlds turn out to be remarkably close. "And so I read on, past my own geography and history. . . . The great writers were not remote. They were in Accrington."[11]

Why Be Happy When You Could Be Normal?—the title of Winterson's memoir—is the bewildered question asked by her adoptive mother on finding out that her daughter is a lesbian. Neither happiness nor normality turns out to be on the cards. The book is a record of woundedness: the scars inflicted by the abusive and eccentric Mrs. Winterson; by having been given up for adoption; by never quite knowing who one is. It is also an account of how stories help make things bearable. As a teenager, Winterson leaves home, sleeps in a Mini, and makes her home in the Accrington public library, reading her way through English literature from A to Z. Allies are at hand: a solicitous librarian; the Dewey decimal system; the comical but informative Mrs. Ratlow (head of English). Through books she forges ties to real and fictional lives, to authors who write and to characters who are written. Personal stories speak to others, she observes, when they become paradigms or parables. "The intensity of a story . . . releases into a bigger space than the one it occupied in time and place. The story crosses the threshold from my world into yours."[12] A transpersonal crossing or connection is achieved. Central to Winterson's text are two forms of aesthetic relation that I'll consider in more detail: *allegiance* (a felt affiliation or solidarity with certain others) and *recognition* (the struggle to know oneself and to be known). "I have always been interested in stories of disguise and mistaken identity, of naming and knowing. How are you recognised? How do you recognise yourself?"[13]

It is hardly surprising that a novelist testifies to the salvific power of stories. Not everyone, of course, will respond along the same lines as Winterson, or in the same way. And glitches and misfirings are all too common; there can be a failure to identify (being bored, distracted, apathetic, irritated, turned off) or a conscious refusal to identify, whether for political, ethical, or other reasons. Countless contingencies are in play. My aim is neither to prescribe nor to prohibit but to redescribe a form of attachment that is often caricatured or poorly understood and to tackle some common canards: that identifying is synonymous with "sameness"; that it involves a naive view of character; that it can only be sappy, sentimental, or unreflective.

CHARACTER AS *UMWELT*

A second aspect of identification is its relation to persons: what readers and viewers identify with, above all, are *characters*.

(Though, as we'll see, this attachment may bleed into a felt affinity with an author, an actor, a situation, a style: audiences are promiscuous in their affections. The question of what it means to connect to a style is one that I discuss in more detail elsewhere, under the rubric of "attunement.")[14] There has been much hand-wringing over the status of character in literary and film studies. The antihumanist orientation of the last few decades led to a pervasive skepticism about the status of fictional persons; critics insisted that characters were nothing but signifiers: textual holograms, verbal phantasms, or visual illusions. As such, they bore no relation to persons; to treat them as such was the epitome of naivety or philistinism. Yet the case is hardly compelling; after all, characters do share qualities with real people, while our interactions with others often draw on insights we have gleaned from novels or films. We translate between fiction and life without blinking.

More recently, critics have taken a different tack, appealing to ideas from evolutionary psychology. Humans, they point out, have an intrinsic bias toward sociability: we are primed to be curious about the thoughts, feelings, and actions of other persons. The draw of fiction is akin to the pleasures of gossip and other forms of bonding. We have evolved to be curious about the motives of others—being able to distinguish between friend and enemy is a competitive advantage that promotes survival—and are drawn to stories that stimulate deep features of our social brains. Such stories teach us to mind-read, to make sense of other people, to hone our interpersonal intelligence. Fiction, for Blakey Vermeule, offers large doses of social information and cognitive stimulation that it would be too costly, dangerous, and difficult for us to extract from the world on our own.[15]

The act of leveling here is vigorous—perhaps a little too vigorous. Is there really such a close correlation between interest in real persons and interest in fictional persons? Is the latter just a shadow or spin-off of the former? The lack of reciprocity in the way we relate to characters is nothing at all like real-world interactions: obsessive book reading might conceivably go along with a *lack* of sociability or social intelligence.[16] Meanwhile, there are other ways in which attachments to characters differ. We can be drawn to fictional figures (de Sade's Juliette, Roquentin, the Underground Man) whose real-world equivalents we would run miles to avoid. Moreover, the affordances of fiction—sneaking into the minds of strangers to capture fragile wisps of thought and feeling; stoking suspense and choreographing crisis—can make fictional figures more vivid, more intensely present, than many of the people around us. They are fascinating not just as prototypes or models for real-world interaction but because of their difference—their aesthetic difference. "A handful of fictional characters," writes Mario Vargas Llosa in his engaging meditation on *Madame Bovary*, "have marked my life more profoundly than a great number of the flesh-and-blood beings I have known."[17]

Emma Bovary is an especially striking case of such fictional attachments. She has been endlessly deciphered by critics; adopted, translated, and reimagined by film directors and artists; invoked by pundits and commentators and absorbed into the French language (*bovarysme*). Her creation is tied to Flaubert's fastidious concern with literary technique; for some critics, she serves as little more than an alibi for parsing the formal features of *indirect style libre*. Yet this technique raises intriguing questions about reader response: does its blend of emotion and distance encourage identification or undercut it? Literary critics have typically stressed distance, vaunting the famed impersonality and detachment of Flaubert's prose. And yet there are also murmuring acknowledgments—and not only from women—of intense affinity and identification. Here is Vargas Llosa again, drawing out the commonalities between himself and Emma: "our incurable materialism, our greater predilection for the pleasures of the body than for those of the soul, our respect for the senses and instinct, our preference for this earthly life over any other."[18]

Neither of the above options fits the bill: hammering home the fictionality of characters in order to render them shadowy and insubstantial; or minimizing their fictionality by treating imaginary and real persons as if they served similar—evolutionary—purposes. Another possibility presents itself: it is their fictional qualities that make characters real. Characters are not real persons; they are real fictional beings! Art is frequently feted, Latour remarks, while being denied any objectivity or ultimate importance; it is seen as significant, yet not really serious. We are in need of ontological fattening therapies, he suggests, so as to endow fictional beings with more substance. These beings "offer us an imagination that we would not have had without them. Don Juan exists as surely as the characters in *Friends*; President Bartlett occupied the White House for some time with more reality than his pale double George W. Bush."[19] Certain figures encountered in novels and films are vivid, memorable, charismatic, arresting, alive, not despite their aesthetic qualities but because of them. They possess a kind of reality that we should cherish and respect; that they are made up does not mean that they do not matter.

That they are fictional, meanwhile, means both more and less than their fictionality is often taken to mean. *More*, in the sense that characters cannot be separated from their aesthetic mediations: identifying with a character can also be a matter of cathecting onto a plot, a situation, a mise-en-scène, a setting, a style. In narratology, character is often treated as a distinct unit; when we consider the phenomenology of response, things become much messier. To what extent can an impulse to identify with Thelma and Louise be disassociated from the sublime landscape that surrounds and enframes them? In what sense is affinity with the hectoring narrator of a Thomas Bernhard novel about identifying with a style as well as a person? Flipping things around, however, characters can also merge into real-world persons; they are *less* than fictional insofar as identifying with a character, as we'll see, may bleed into attachment to an author or a movie star. Divisions between what is inside and outside the text are often transgressed, overlooked, or ignored.

Fictional characters, moreover, are not stuck fast to the works in which they first appear. Like Emma Bovary, characters may refuse to stay put; they survive adaptation, hopping from literature to film to graphic novel, wresting themselves free of the words out of which they were first made. A figure with a walk-on part in one novel may pop up as the central protagonist of another. *Wide Sargasso Sea* is the most well-known example of this "minor-character genre," but recent years have seen a slew of new novels recounting the fate of *Ahab's Wife* or *Mr. Dalloway*.[20] The proliferation of fan fictions in recent decades, meanwhile, testifies to the highly translatable aspects of characters, their potential to be reborn in new contexts. Such fiction, Francesca Coppa remarks, poses "what if" questions about characters: What if Sherlock Holmes were a Harlem crime fighter? What if Bilbo Baggins were queer? Characters are not just transposed but transformed: kitted out with new traits, moved into alternate worlds.[21] It is not only boundaries between texts that are porous but boundaries between texts and everyday life. Joyce's portly protagonist is resurrected in literary festivities every June 16; young people around the world don striped scarves and metamorphose into Harry Potter or Hermione Granger; Carrie Bradshaw beckons from a magazine or beams from the cosmetics counter. Sherlock Holmes, the object of countless biographies and histories, has recently been reincarnated in the TV series *Sherlock*, and we can now, courtesy of Daniel Mallory Ortberg, read phone texts from Jane Eyre.[22]

Characters are movable, teleporting into new media and milieus, times and places. They swarm among us, populating the world with their idiosyncrasies, accessories, trademarks, sidekicks, and sayings. They are not just inside books, awaiting our attention to spring to life, but also outside books, beings we may bump into without expecting it. They differ from persons yet are easily recognizable as akin to persons, objects of widespread devotion (or dislike). In short, they form part of an

Umwelt. In contrast to the mechanistic associations of a "context" that bears down on us, the idea of *Umwelt* seeks to convey the dynamic and open-ended nature of a being's relation to its surroundings, which it customizes in particular ways. We act on this *Umwelt*—that is, surrounding world—in interacting with it; the environment as it concerns us is a networked array of phenomena. Characters matter to *us* and yet are not simply "in our minds"; they come to us as if from elsewhere; they possess a degree of solidity, permanence, and force.[23]

It is here that formalist theories of character come up short, in their failure to account for the felt vitality of fictional beings. The world would look very different without Jekyll and Hyde, Faust, Antigone, Mary Poppins, Norman Bates, Dracula, Nancy Drew, Don Juan, Spock, Hedda Gabler, Oedipus, Winnie the Pooh, Scrooge, Darth Vader, Hercule Poirot, HAL, Mickey Mouse, the Simpsons, Alice, Medea, Scrooge, Gandalf, Sam Spade, Anna Karenina. These figures are not just bundles of signifiers; they are worldly actors haloed with affective and existential force. Historical theories, meanwhile, often strive to rein in character by restricting and limiting its reach: defining it as a literary device tied to the genre of the eighteenth- and nineteenth-century European novel. Yet the reality that radiates from fictional beings does not depend on the conventions of realism: some of the most vivid exemplars come from fantasy, science fiction, stories for children, Greek and Renaissance tragedy, and tales of divinities. Of course, the sense of what it means to be a person fluctuates over time: philosophies of individualism, changing religious and political ideas, legal categories, the rise of human sciences such as psychology and psychoanalysis all play their part. Fictional persons evolve accordingly, as new forms and genres grapple with these changes. Yet characters can also cut across historical and cultural boundaries: that Medea has survived the long trek from a Greek amphitheater to a Pasolini film set suggests the limits of a certain kind of contextual explanation.

Another important thing to be kept in mind: although characters are fictional beings, they cannot be quarantined from historical persons who make claims on our attention. In *The Bell Jar*, for example, it is virtually impossible to disentangle the protagonist from the long shadow cast by Sylvia Plath. And here second-wave feminism played a decisive role, as a social movement linked to literature from the start. Feminist novels often strengthened ties between female characters, authors, and readers by deliberately blurring distinctions between fiction and autobiography. Many of these ties are still sustained in women-only book clubs, college courses devoted to women's writing, the marketing of female-centered genres ranging from chick lit to feminist fantasy. They are woven out of the passions and obsessions of readers, the diffuse yet still powerful aftershocks of a social movement, and the calculations and guesses of publishers, which may hit the jackpot or entirely miss the mark.

Yet we should not conclude that a so-called "identity politics" is the source of all author-character confusions. Elena Ferrante has attracted a passionate cohort of feminist readers drawn to her Naples trilogy and its portrayal of female friendship across class differences. Yet when she was outed in 2016—her cover blown by a zealous Italian journalist—many of these same feminist readers responded with outrage and a sense of violation. Here was a case where the author's separation from her writings—her refusal to give credence to autobiographical readings—was to be respected. Meanwhile, Karl Ove Knausgård is a writer who moves fluidly in and out of the pages of his own text, such that the distinction between fiction and autobiography no longer makes sense. The seven volumes of *My Struggle* include numerous feedback loops between work and life; aggrieved reactions to Knausgård's no-holds-barred account are folded back into the work being written and trigger a new wave of commentary and reaction; the author's celebrity, nationally and internationally, affects the way in which his first-person narrator is perceived. *My Struggle* is widely acclaimed as a work of literature rather than just a well-written autobiography—

and yet author and protagonist blur into one.[24] The "death of the author" thesis—a ubiquitous slogan in literary studies for several decades—has come to seem increasingly outdated, as authors become ever more visible, voluble, and inescapable. They give interviews, hold forth on blogs or Twitter, opine on the latest political events, talk back to prize committees, appear in full or half-empty auditoriums—not titans to be worshiped but promoters of their work and participants in numerous networks.

A crossover of another kind occurs when viewing a film: responses to fictional figures are mixed up with reactions to the persons who play them. (One of the 1940s film fans interviewed by Jackie Stacey remarked: "I was completely lost; it wasn't Ginger Rogers dancing with Fred Astaire, it was me.")[25] In the theater, actors are physically present yet are subsumed by their characters; in the movie theater, actors are physically absent, yet they subsume their characters (we decide to see the new film featuring Tilda Swinton). "The character in a film," remarks Erwin Panofsky, "lives and dies with the actor."[26] Not invariably, of course—experimental and avant-garde films strive to block such forms of identification. Yet the claim often holds true, with the entanglement of character and actor being carried over into multiple venues—any high school performance of *The Sound of Music* will call up the specter of Julie Andrews. Meanwhile, images encountered on the cinema screen are haloed with factoids, BuzzFeed interviews, magazine articles, and other films in which a star has appeared. This spillover creates a many-layered text, in which character and star image may harmonize, overlap, or conflict. (As an instance of the latter, Richard Dyer cites *Gentlemen Prefer Blondes*, where the cynical gold-digger persona of Lorelei clashes with the guileless sexuality radiating from Marilyn Monroe.)[27] Viewers cannot revert to a state of ignorance or innocence; the penumbra of associations around Nicole Kidman or Gérard Depardieu can markedly affect the textures of response.

Characters, in short, are portmanteau creatures, assembled out of disparate materials drawn from fiction and life. Rather than being restricted to a single text, they often serve as nodes in many networks. They are distributed, adapted, and mediated. Their presence can be exceptionally vivid, yet it is painstakingly composed. We might say, drawing from Hélène Mialet's analysis of the public persona of Stephen Hawking, that characters are *incorporated*.[28] They are fabricated out of many things working together: the texts that house them; random scraps of knowledge about authors or actors; acculturation into ways of reading and habits of response; the diligence and devotion of publishers, producers, agents, reviewers, fans; the fictional objects with which they are associated (Sherlock Holmes's pipe; Jane Eyre's gray dress) and the real objects they bring into the world, from Harry Potter wands to Don Quixote prints.

And in identifying with characters, we connect *through* them to other persons and to things. As Jon Najarian points out, "from film-screenings and book-releases to comic-cons and quidditch matches, characters can encourage us to form social ties with other, non-fictional human beings." In some instances, as we'll see in the case of *Thelma and Louise*, such group identifications can have a dramatic impact, fanning out into the public sphere to shape attitudes and ideas. Characters also mediate our relations to stuff, most obviously in the case of commercial spin-offs (*Thelma and Louise* T-shirts) but also in relation to all kinds of souvenirs, mementos, fetishes, totems, tokens, love objects. When the house of Leopold and Molly Bloom was demolished in 1967, Joyceans rushed to preserve it but could salvage only the front door, which is now displayed in the James Joyce Center in Dublin. It has become part of a network of Joycean entanglements. Looking at it implants a vague sense of melancholy, Najarian writes. "You may realize that this never was a door of ingress or of egress for Leopold Bloom: neither he, nor Molly, nor Stephen, nor the pussens, ever walked through this door, ever listened to it creak. Bloom never remembered, standing in front of *this* door, that he had forgotten to remember his keys and found himself locked out. . . . And yet, although Leopold Bloom never walked through the door that is housed currently at 35 North Great George's Street, that does not mean that he never lived."[29]

To live in this fashion, characters must rely on the kindness of strangers; without the input of readers or viewers, they are naught. Yet the latter are also obligated to the fictional beings that take possession of them, infiltrate them, speak through them. Stripped of the sediments of the novels I've read, the films and TV shows I've watched, I would be another person entirely. Fictional beings serve as alter egos, ideal types, negative exempla, moral guides, objects of desire, imaginary friends. They depend on us yet also engender us. Characters encountered in fiction often cross over into other contexts; they can linger in the mind after a book is finished, readers have reported, interacting with them in daily life in a vivid, even hallucinatory fashion.[30] Here again, we see how characters are taken up into an *Umwelt*. As Latour writes, fictional beings "have this peculiarity, then; their objectivity depends on their being reprised, taken up again by subjectivities that would not exist themselves if these beings had not given them to us."[31]

An objection, meanwhile, has been gathering force: surely such talk about identifying is far more relevant to some texts than to others. Does it make any sense in relation to the milestones of modernism? These works, after all, dealt a death blow to character—that is to say, the creation of well-rounded fictional persons, kitted out with extended families, parlors, mustaches, and hats, who marched through the endless detours and byways of Victorian novels to a satisfying finale. We might think of the celebrated modernist counterexamples: Musil's "man without qualities," the multivoiced ebb and flow of Woolf's *The Waves*, the blank-faced ciphers that populate the writings of Kafka and Beckett. For Adorno, the import of modernism lay in its exposure of the anachronism of character. Individuality, he declared, had been liquidated by the historical and political upheavals of the twentieth century. To cling to notions of the person in a world of standardization and commodification was nothing more than sentimental illusion, the stuff of cheap biographical literature.[32] Bolstered in recent years by poststructuralist skepticism about selfhood, this view of modernism as dissolving character is a recurring thread in literary studies.

Julian Murphet has recently restated the case with vigor, elaborating on the ties between modernism and multiplicity. Not just the instability but the impossibility of character, he argues, are vividly actualized in the architecture of modernist form. In the works of Joyce, Proust, and Woolf the very idea of character is shredded, dissolved, and washed away, as unity gives way to a multiplicity of shifting and unstable identities. Adamant that modernist fiction breaks with everything that came before, Murphet is unwilling to acknowledge continuities between modernism and its precursors. He also waves away—as merely pragmatic—questions of how readers engage with fictional persons.[33] Yet such questions cannot so peremptorily be pushed aside; works come into being only insofar as they are actualized by readers or viewers. Here Hans-Robert Jauss's response to Adorno seems apropos: "interpretation that bypasses this primary aesthetic experience is the arrogance of a philologist who subscribes to the error that the text was not created for readers, but for him."[34] No one would dispute that fictional figures look different in *Mrs. Dalloway* than in *Middlemarch*—a difference marked in the unspooling of plot, the rendering of dialogue, the fracturing of time, the very different capturing of mental states. Yet this does not mean that person schemas drop out of sight or that readers do not form ties to figures in modernist fiction. The twofoldedness of character—as both person and aesthetic device—is manifest in both Eliot and Woolf, though in differing ways. And if we keep in mind the other ties we've looked at—to authors, film actors, etc.—we might want to make a case not just for the twofoldedness of character but for its *multifoldedness*.[35]

Rebecca Solnit has written about her difficulties appreciating *Lolita* in the light of her empathy for the heroine. One of her readers responded with a testy reprimand: "To read Lolita and 'identify' with one of the characters is to entirely misunderstand Nabokov."[36] What to make of this interchange? As this reader suggests, Nabokov was notoriously dismissive of any desire to identify; his verbal pyrotechnics and layers of irony sought to school readers in a different kind of literary response. And yet the claim that the works of Nabokov—or other examples of stylized, ironic, or rebarbative fiction, whether by Kafka or Kathy Acker—have abolished or done away with identification might give us pause. The claim only holds, I am suggesting, if we adhere to an overly schematic idea of what it means to identify. After all, the indignant reader who responded to Solnit by rallying to Nabokov's defense is hardly free of attachment—perhaps he does not identify with one of *Lolita*'s characters, but he is certainly identifying with *something*. An author? A work? A style? A text-person composite? The gap between himself and Solnit may not be as wide as he thinks.

STRANDS OF IDENTIFICATION

A sharpening of terms is overdue. What exactly is going on when we identify? What kinds of attachments are being forged? I share the view of film scholar Murray Smith that identifying is not one thing but differing things that occur in many combinations. In the following pages, I draw on some of his ideas— while reformatting them in ways he might not sanction—in order to disentangle four strands of identification: alignment, allegiance, recognition, and empathy.[37] Less exhaustive than they are suggestive, these terms can give us a better handle on how films and novels reel in audiences—how they solicit our devotion and our care.

Alignment refers to the formal means by which texts shape a reader's or viewer's access to character: the part played by the work rather than its audience. (It is, in this sense, akin to the idea of "focalization" in narrative theory.) It points to the directive force of narrative, description, and point of view: whose decisions or desires drive a plot; which figures are depicted in scrupulous detail; whose perspective we are invited to adopt. Some characters bask in the ambient warmth of the novel's attention, while other are relegated to a Siberian wasteland; we are made privy to every rueful reflection or flutter of desire in the mind of X, while the inner life of Y remains utterly beyond reach. Alignment thus resonates with familiar ways of talking about fiction: major and minor characters, round and flat. How a work directs its focus can strongly affect its power to resonate with particular audiences—or fail to do so. It can also hook up to larger patterns of amplified attention or neglect; that attention to character is striated by social inequality and sanctioned ignorance is by now a familiar point within criticism.

Of course, to center a novel or a film on a character's perspective is not to endorse that perspective, as an unruly throng of unreliable narrators makes clear. In responding to characters, we draw on various sources: accounts of their actions or motivations; judgments by other characters; textual cues, whether implicit (hinting at a character's mental state by panning across a disorderly room; using chiaroscuro lighting to conjure up feelings of dread) or explicit (naming a figure Cruella De Vil). A piling up of discrepancies and evasions often indicates that a character is misrepresenting, misreading, or misevaluating, that their words are not to be taken at face value. Scholars of narratology have expended much energy on this question; *The Remains of the Day*, especially, has been pored over by critics eager to parse the various techniques used by Ishiguro to cast doubt on the first-person account of his self-deceiving butler. Alignment may or may not encourage identification: narratives offer varying blends of reliability and unreliability, intimacy and distance.

Yet we must also keep in mind that films and novels are not tyrants commanding their subjects on pain of death—other

forces are also in play, creating distractions, offering coun-
tersuggestions, running interference. Alignment is only one
aspect of the puzzle of identification; the formal features of a
work invite audiences to respond in certain ways but cannot
impel them to do so. A dislike of a particular film star; a critical
essay read in college; a felt affinity with a minor character or a
villain; the impact of a trenchant or excoriating review—there
are numerous reasons why audiences do not fall into line and
may identify in a haphazard or unpredictable fashion. It is entirely possible to see oneself as Casaubon rather than Dorothea,
to identify with Archie Bunker rather than seeing him as a sa-
tiric foil. "Bad fans" are all too frequent—audiences who fail to
honor a work's intent, whether willfully or unknowingly.[38] It is
here that film theory, at a certain moment, went off the rails,
not in highlighting recurring formal patterns in movies (such
as the asymmetry between who looks and who is looked at) but
in seizing on such patterns as clinching evidence of how audiences identify or—even worse—of their overall psychological
makeup or political beliefs. The text, in short, was hailed as the
sole actor; all other actors and intermediaries, mishaps and ser-
endipities, were airbrushed out of the scene

Allegiance speaks to the question of how ethical or political values—that is, acts of evaluating—draw audiences closer
to some figures rather than others. It is a familiar idea that art,
in modernity, has sought to wrest itself free from moral prescriptions; a distinguished roll call of censored writers, from
the marquis de Sade to Henry Miller, have lobbed hand gre-
nades at religious and social pieties. Thanks to this history,
no critic nowadays would praise a novel or a film by dubbing
it "moral"—a language now used only by the Christian Right.
And yet, that art provokes established values does not mean it
floats free of value; excoriations of bourgeois hypocrisy or en-
demic racism carry their own normative force; ethical as well as
political judgments are in play. In experiences of both art and
life, it is impossible to escape frameworks of value: as Steven

Connor points out, we cannot help orienting ourselves to what we take to be the better rather than the worse.[39] The "is" cannot be disentangled from the "ought"; matters of fact are mixed up with matters of concern. And here there are countless crossings between the modes of aesthetics, ethics, and politics; attempts to purify these modes by keeping them entirely separate are an exercise in futility.

Allegiance, then, is in play whenever we find ourselves siding with a character and what we take that character to stand for—an allegiance that can, of course, be partial, qualified, or ambivalent. Such acts of evaluating affect what audiences perceive and how they respond, shaping assessments of character and situation. An attachment may be brief—lasting only the length of a novel or film—or it may have a lasting effect on our perception of how things are. Such ethical engagement does not rule out critical estrangement, as Carl Plantinga points out—but it is often tied to an experience of immersion in a fictional world that film theory has failed to take seriously.[40]

Here we might look to *Thelma and Louise*: a film that inspired passionate arguments and became a touchstone of public debate. The film serves as a striking example of collective identification: where individual reactions were heavily mediated by larger patterns of response. To express an opinion on *Thelma and Louise* was to take up a position in an extended network of relations, a heavily trafficked zone of analysis, argument, and conflicts about values. The film triggered strong responses and partisan commentary; it did not simply speak to preexisting groups but called these groups into being. Via their responses, viewers defined themselves as fans or skeptics, as antifeminist or as subscribing to differing kinds of feminism. In their reactions to *Thelma and Louise*, many viewers came to see themselves as part of a "we": a virtual feminist community formed via a shared devotion to a film and what it stood for. They became attached to a film that in turn connected them to others and to shared convictions.

Why did this film about a waitress and a housewife on the lam forge such enduring ties? Surely because these ties were woven out of multiple strands: the mythic resonance of classic film genres (the road movie, the female friendship film, the Western) blended in unprecedented ways; a widespread hunger for new female character types and the film industry's willingness to capitalize on this demand; the dazzle of Hollywood names with both artistic credibility and wide appeal (Ridley Scott, Susan Sarandon); and, not least, the forging of ties between aesthetic and political representation. It is only at certain moments—thanks to the rise of new social movements and what came to be known as "cultural politics"—that fictional portrayals of women and minorities are scrutinized as a revealing index of their overall status in society.[41] A film is no longer either enjoyed or else dismissed without further thought; rather, it is painstakingly *deciphered*—not only by academics but also by audiences at the Cineplex—for what it conveys about equality or inequality, inclusion or exclusion. The 1970s saw the emergence of what I've called a feminist counter-public sphere, a space of public debate about newly compelling and contentious topics: women in the workplace, sexuality, motherhood, harassment, sexist images.[42] This sphere inspired fresh ways of interpreting and also cathecting onto works of art: practices of critique, along with a widespread yearning for new female-centered imaginaries. And in this context, *Thelma and Louise* became a flashpoint for strong attachments and heated arguments; as was repeatedly said, the film "struck a nerve."

The impulse to identify—or not—with Susan Sarandon and Geena Davis was thoroughly entangled with questions of value. What was the ethical import of a story line in which women were transformed into outlaws after shooting a rapist? Did it matter that most of the male characters were portrayed as buffoons or scoundrels? What was the film saying about female camaraderie and love between women? Its heroines were widely seen as icons of female rebellion, and yet responses did not always fall along predictable lines. Sheila Benson, writing in the *Los Angeles Times*, declared *Thelma and Louise* a betrayal of feminism in espousing revenge rather than "responsibility, equality, sensitivity, and understanding." Echoing similar sentiments, Margaret Carlson in *Time* underscored the difficulties of allegiance: "it becomes harder and harder to root for the heroines, who make the wrong choice at every turn and act more like Clint Eastwood than Katherine Hepburn."[43] Conversely, while male viewers often dismissed or disparaged the film, others saw it several times, claiming that it had galvanized and transformed them.[44]

The messy realities of such responses contravene what were once axioms of film theory. Women do not always identify with women; meanwhile, some men connect with female figures across gender lines, finding other points of affinity or relation. Moreover, acts of identifying, while they can be emotional, even passionate, are also *reflective*: they are informed by beliefs, ideals, and values. It is a matter not just of feeling but of thinking. As Kim Chabot Davis points out in an illuminating reception study of Jane Campion's art-house melodrama *The Piano*, identifying is not just an unconscious or subliminal activity; it is shaped by how audiences assess characters and evaluate situations, by their core commitments and their consciously held beliefs. And here ethical and political affiliations can inspire wildly variant reactions. In the case of both *The Piano* and *Thelma and Louise*, conflicting views of feminism—not just whether viewers saw themselves as feminist but what they took feminism to *mean*—had a decisive impact on whether and how viewers identified. Was feminism a matter of equality or freedom, of reclaiming femaleness or rejecting it, of real-world goals or utopian dreams? Political ideas and beliefs served as key mediators, shaping what audiences cared about, their affective reactions, and the texture of their response.[45]

Of course, other kinds of values were also in play. Some of the above-cited objections to *Thelma and Louise* may sound overly literal, assessing characters as moral exemplars rather than fictional beings. The draw of the film surely had much to do with a comeuppance that was fundamentally aesthetic in nature. *Thelma and Louise* was a riposte to a history of impoverished plotlines, a corrective to a restricted repertoire of roles for women. That audiences delighted in its narrative reversals and appropriation of masculine symbols (cars, guns) spoke to a sharpening public realization of how severely gender norms had constrained possibilities of character and plot. The film helped forge a new tonal repertoire for women's films: a mood of defiance, rebellion, and exuberance that is underscored by the physical as well as mental metamorphosis of the main characters, including the shedding of restrictive feminine clothing and a freer, more forceful body language. Now that female action heroes are commonplace, it is hard to realize the audaciousness of such a tonal shift—and the riskiness of a screenplay that fell outside the marketing templates of its time and almost didn't get filmed.[46] When critics worried that audience identification with Thelma and Louise would trigger direct imitation— acts of real-world violence by women against men—they were relying on an overly simple notion of what it means to identify.

Meanwhile, another kind of complaint—that the film was antifeminist in portraying female independence as leading to death—also seems a tad overliteral. The film ends with the heroines driving their turquoise Thunderbird off the edge of a cliff and soaring over the Grand Canyon: are they committing suicide or taking flight? Screenwriter Callie Khouri drily notes: "We left them in mid-air. That wasn't because they ran out of film."[47] Here, as elsewhere, *Thelma and Louise* meshes the political with the existential-symbolic: Ridley Scott's spectacular shots of desert landscapes and canyons tie his characters to a visual language of the sublime—a sense of overpowering awe and magnitude—that has usually been the province of men. This visual backdrop endows their condition as women on the run with a metaphysical weight and substance; soaring into the sky, they join a mythological cohort of airborne women. As Louise pushes down on the accelerator and the women grip hands, the film's final moments convey their sheer undauntedness—an unflinching facing-up-to-death—and female solidarity.

That some critics chose to assess the film as a blueprint for real-world behavior rather than a flight of the imagination, meanwhile, is not an argument against allegiance as such. After all, those who passionately defended *Thelma and Louise* were also taking a stand; siding with it against one-sided interpretations, reaching for another critical language that was based on fantasy rather than mimesis; defending the flawed complexities of its heroines against attempts to flatten them into man-haters or feminist role models. A pushback against reductive readings is also an ethical position: defending a work of art against those who would cram it into a preexisting box. Allegiances, in short, are always in play. Poetics borrows from ethics, writes Paul Ricoeur, even when calling for a suspension or ironic inversion of ethical judgments; fiction serves as an ethical laboratory that allows for all kinds of experimentation with values.[48] *Thelma and Louise* is a striking example of such a value experiment, its effects still traceable a quarter of a century later.

Murray Smith introduces *recognition* to account for the apprehension of a gestalt: how we come to see pixels on a screen (or black marks on a page) as adding up to human figures. Viewers rely on perceptual cues (especially body, face, and voice) to distinguish human agents from other aspects of a film and to understand them as being individuated and continuous. Recognition is thus, Smith proposes, the most basic level of engagement with a film; it is a precondition for the audience's ability to follow and make sense of a narrative—though one that can be flouted by avant-garde film—and to respond emotionally to characters. Smith does not tackle, however, what strikes me as a more interesting question: recognition as an aspect of identification. In contrast to a base-level ability to recognize all characters *as* characters, such a response is selective; one recognizes oneself in certain characters rather than in others. On what grounds? And what does it mean to see aspects of oneself in a film or a novel? Whereas allegiance involves ethical or political values and empathy is about co-feeling, recognition names an experience of *coming to know*: of being struck by some kind of insight or realization. (Such knowing may, of course, have an ethical, political, or emotional spin-off.)

And here the forms of self-knowing afforded by aesthetic recognition are more unpredictable and complex than they are often taken to be. Critical theorists have often derided experiences of recognition in art, equating them with a sense of complacency and an endorsement of the commonplace. And yet "recognition is not repetition: it denotes not just the previously known, but the becoming known. . . . In a mobile play of interiority and exteriority, something that exists outside of me inspires a revised or altered sense of who I am."[49] Glimpsing aspects of oneself in fictional beings involves a volatile mix of the familiar and the different; to recognize is to know again but also to see afresh. As I recognize myself in another, I also learn something about myself. And I may be startled or discomfited by what I see.

In an earlier book I discussed how self-recognition can link up to struggles for social recognition: that Ibsen's female audience identified with the repressed rage of Hedda Gabler, for example, was not just a matter of individual response but helped fan the sparks of the early suffragette movement. Self-recognition (a woman seeing aspects of her own situation in Hedda's) linked up to a call for public acknowledgment (women demanding to be recognized as equal agents in the world). I now want to consider a different kind of self-recognition—one that is harder to leverage in terms of any discernible political use value—as it relates to the work of Austrian novelist Thomas Bernhard, acknowledged master of the tirade, the diatribe, the rant. A typical Bernhard novel consists of a single unbroken paragraph of insults, invectives, and exaggerations spewing from the mouth of a monomaniac narrator. Its language is repetitive, relentless, incantatory, spiraling obsessively around the same ideas and phrases. Bernhard's writing is often described as absolutist, dogmatic, solipsistic, and hyperbolic; he is hailed as an exaggeration artist, a madman of exasperated orality.

Bernhard is an illuminating case for rethinking certain commonplaces about identification. There is, first of all, the relentless negativity of his writing: an oceanic heave of venom, disgust, bitterness, and loathing. If readers are identifying with something, this "something" has little to do with affection or positive emotions. The lure of the rant lies in its destructive and self-destructive qualities, its hectoring and haranguing, its push toward extremity—what Robert Cohen calls its bilious, scorched-earth quality. Cohen writes beautifully of "the giddy drunken music of obsession, that agitated, overstated letting-go, which pushes us viscerally to the edge of our conditioned responses, and then asks us to follow our deepest, most self-annihilating instincts and plunge with it over that edge, into god knows what."[50]

As these words suggest, one effect of the Bernhardian rant is to batter the edifice of individuality. Sound takes precedence over sense; selfhood sags and sways under the torrential force of words gone wild; the reader is bludgeoned by repetition heaped on repetition, by a flood of verbal tics and manic twitches. Language churns relentlessly, as if without human intervention; readers find themselves trapped in what feels like an automatic writing machine. Bernhard's famous nested sentences—one character recounts the words of another in stylistically indistinguishable prose—have the effect of confusing frames of narration, such that it is often difficult to discern who is speaking: "Glenn locked himself up in his North American cage, I in my Upper Austrian one, Wertheimer said, I thought. He with his alomania, I with my desperation. All three with our desperation, he said, I thought."[51] The typical scenario of a Bernhard novel is a trio of figures who refract each other's obsessions: the logic is spatial rather than temporal, a closed field of repetition and imprisoning reflections rather than an open-ended plot.

And yet, despite its disdain for character development and literary realism, its aggression and misanthropy, Bernhard's work inspires intense and ardent identification. (There is even talk of a Bernhard cult.) His influence on the work of W. G. Sebald is frequently noted, but there are many other disciples. Geoff Dyer's *Out of Sheer Rage*, a meditation on writing—or failing to write—a book about D. H. Lawrence, is thoroughly Bernhardian in its prose style, as is much of the work of novelist Tim Parks. There is the explicit homage—or is it pastiche?—of *Revulsion: Thomas Bernhard in San Salvador*, whose vituperative narrator spews indiscriminate insults at every aspect of Salvadoran life, from its corrupt universities to its revolting cuisine. (Its author, Horacio Castellanos Moya, received death threats after the book's publication.) Even Bernhard's reviewers become infected, as in this *Village Voice* commentary by Gary Indiana:

> In those years when Bernhard was writing *The Loser*, *Old Masters*, *Woodcutters*, and finally *Extinction*, I lived in a country where the obvious truth of Bernhard's writing was intolerable, a country where a writer like Bernhard or Sartre or Gombrowicz would only be reviled as a nest-fouler, a raging disease of a country bent on becoming Disney World, a country of advanced senility, a malignant nation of putrid happy endings, a country ruled by malevolent dwarfs, a country intoxicated by technology, a country crawling with desperate hypocrites, spiritually no different than Austria.[52]

For Indiana, Bernhard's excoriations of Austria call to mind the United States, a country equally well stocked with "desperate hypocrites." The two writers share a loathing for putrid happy endings; the baffled and impotent rage of the Bernhardian narrator echoes Indiana's own. Identification does not depend on literary realism or mimetic accuracy; truth can also lie in excess and exaggeration; affiliations can form around kernels of antisocial venom and apoplectic spleen.

I admit to being infected by the same virus and only narrowly escaped the fate of a Bernhard dissertation; returning to his work feels like picking a scab, the characters' obsessions rubbing in my own. What should we call this form of attachment? Empathy, with its associations of care, concern, and tolerance, seems like entirely the wrong word here. (Tolerance! A laughable idea in the Thomas Bernhard universe.) Identification-as-recognition, then, but not via any kind of sociological or even psychological matching. I am not an Austrian man, share little of the background of Bernhard or his characters, and am, if anything, rather conflict averse. And yet there is something in Bernhard that resonates, that feels familiar. "Affective situation" is a phrase coined by Ethan Reed to capture the diffuseness of certain affects as they splay across self and world, transpersonal patterns of response forged out of various things working together.[53]

What I share with Bernhard, I want to say, is an *irritation situation*. By temperament I am something of a malcontent, prone to bouts of brooding and seething. There is something exceptionally gratifying about Bernhard's channeling of this irritation: the cathartic relief of seeing it acknowledged, cranked up a hundredfold, and vomited out into the world. Recognition meets up with a pleasure in vicarious expression. And yet, in its sheer hyperbole and lack of discrimination, its flagrant contradictions and digressions, the Bernhardian rant teeters on the edge of absurdity. To rave about the stupidity and self-righteousness of others is inevitably to drive home one's own stupidity and self-righteousness. The manic energy of Bernhard's prose is exhilarating yet also estranging; the mirror it offers does not flatter. In recognizing my rage against idiocy, I am confronted with the idiocy of my own rage.

Meanwhile, what exactly am I identifying with? Bernhard? Bernhard's first-person narrator? The characters? The seductive-coercive pull of his incantatory sentences? It seems impossible to nail down any definitive answer. A certain kind of critical response would focus on language alone, yet the force of this language lies in conveying a certain attitude. Excessive feelings and categorical judgments are constantly in play, pointing back to a recognizable—if luridly magnified—disposition. What is a Bernhard protagonist if not the quintessential *bad-mouther* and *faultfinder*? Person schemas, even if stylized, exaggerated, and caricatured, are very much in play. And here the characters echo the compulsions of the narrator; the narrator brings to mind the author, with his notorious and vitriolic attacks on the Austrian establishment ("this tiny state is a gigantic dung-hill"); meanwhile, neither Bernhard nor his characters can be disentangled from the remorseless rhythms of his unmistakable prose. Author, characters, and words blur together to form a composite site of attachment. We are dealing, once again, with hybrids, with text-person combinations. Identifying involves a response not only to fictional figures but also to the overall atmosphere of a text as created by its style. Recognition in Bernhard is both personal (character based) *and* transpersonal (a linguistic-aesthetic relation).

I turn, finally, to *empathy*: sharing someone's feelings and responding with concern to these feelings. As we can see, this definition splits into two parts—feeling *with* someone and feeling *for* someone—that are not automatically connected. Analytical philosophers like to cite the example of a torturer getting inside his victim's psyche in order to apply pain-inducing techniques more effectively; he is feeling with, they argue, but certainly not feeling for. Conversely, we can care or feel for a character without experiencing their emotions or mimicking their affective state. (When the hardworking Boxer is carted off to the slaughterhouse in *Animal Farm*, the horse's joyful expectation of retirement is not echoed by the book's readers but only heightens the pathos of his fate.) Yet the solution that is sometimes proposed—a strict separation of empathy from sympathy—seems unsustainable, given their entanglement in everyday usage. To refer to someone as empathic is to convey not just that they are aware of others' feelings but also that they respond to these feelings in a compassionate manner. (More than other strands of identification, empathy is tied to acknowledgment of suffering: feeling and responding to the pain of others.)[54]

It is here that literature—with its ability to stick us inside the minds of strangers—is hailed as a force for the greater good. Empathy has received far more attention than other aspects of identification. "There is a surprising level of agreement," Anne Jurecic writes, "from educators to politicians and philosophers, and even talk show hosts, that *reading literature* makes us more empathic."[55] Feeling a sense of empathy with fictional persons, according to Richard Rorty and Martha Nussbaum, can expand the limits of experience, engender a sense of solidarity with distant others, and do valuable civic and political work. Since the eighteenth century, literary empathy has been hailed as a means of encouraging altruism and of binding readers into a community—working against strong social and economic pressures toward egoism and self-interest. Empathy is also a gendered term: that women are more empathic than men is taken for granted in daily life, popular commentary, and much psychology and neuroscience.

Critical theorists have taken a rather different view, arguing that empathy is soaked through with power and privilege; reading a novel may delude affluent Westerners that they know what it's like to be a slum dweller in Mumbai. Meanwhile, in stressing the role of emotion—I feel, therefore I am—empathy promotes a sentimental and overly simplified understanding of social relations. Jurecic references a number of arguments along these lines, including a feminist critique of *Reading Lolita in Tehran* that accuses the best-selling memoir of divorcing affect from analysis and thus promoting "neoliberal feminism and U.S. imperialism."[56] Here we see echoes of the Brechtian distrust of identification: the conviction that emotions—or at least softer emotions such as empathy—block critical thinking and are complicit with inequality and injustice.

This pushback carries a certain force: the claim that reading literature engenders empathy, which in turn promotes social solidarity, teeters on a shaky platform of assumptions. As we've seen, empathy is not always a motive for reading or the most salient aspect of reading. It is more pertinent to some genres and some readers than others; meanwhile, it remains an open question whether empathy with fictional characters has long-term effects on behavior. And yet denouncing empathy seems no better than idealizing it: no less closed off to the variability and messiness of reader response. And while empathy has its limits, a lack of empathy—a turning away from the perspectives and the pain of others—is hardly a preferable alternative. My former student Kiley Garrett offers another take: "reading a book from another person's perspective may not prompt readers to act altruistically, but it might cause them to think more openly."[57] Repeated exposure to differing forms of life may have a gradual, subtle, or inadvertent effect—even if readers can't point to a specific text that changed their way of thinking. Lines of causality are hard to pin down, and the "impact factor" of literature is exceptionally difficult to measure—yet a world without imaginative fiction would be a very different world.

Here we might look to a review of Mohsin Hamid's *Exit West* by fellow novelist Viet Thanh Nguyen. Published in 2017, *Exit West* follows the lives of a couple, Saeed and Nadia, as their country—unnamed, sketched only in the broadest strokes—descends into civil war and chaos. Electricity and water are cut off; bombs explode on the streets; public executions become routine. Saeed and Nadia struggle to sustain some shreds of their daily existence, until normality is no longer possible and survival becomes their only goal: "for one minute we are pottering about our normal existence and the next minute we are dying."[58] Doors mysteriously begin to appear in apartment buildings and parking lots: magic portals that allow Saeed, Nadia, and their compatriots to step into other countries and start new lives in London or Mykonos or Marin County. Hailed as intruders, they must grapple with hostility and contempt, with the deployment of troops and tanks. Parallels with the Syrian refugee crisis are evident but not belabored. The novel focuses less on geopolitical realities than on conditions of displacement ("that summer it seemed to Saeed and Nadia that the whole planet was on the move") and on how such displacement alters the bond between Nadia and Saeed, forcing them into proximity yet also rendering them strangers to one another.[59]

As Nguyen notes, *Exit West* engages in a delicate balancing act between sameness and difference. Its main characters are educated city dwellers; the textures of their everyday lives—smart phones, recreational drugs, dinners in Chinese restaurants, seminars on "corporate identity and product branding"—connect them to the novel's most likely readers. And yet in other respects—Saeed's insistence on sexual abstinence and devotion to prayer, Nadia's donning of a long black robe to ward off advances from strangers—differences are made manifest. Portraying catastrophe at a slight remove, the text refuses to linger on the spectacle of suffering. (The magic-portal device deflects attention away from the all-too-familiar stories of deadly refugee journeys that permeate the media.) Meanwhile, the crystalline simplicity of Hamid's prose and the quasi-allegorical portrayal of his characters' travails invite readers to place themselves in a related position. Such a stretching of experience, Nguyen suggests, can alter how people feel about refugees. "The reader, of course, must think about what would happen if her own normal life was suddenly, unexpectedly upended by war." In this scenario, empathy with characters does not rule out critical reflection but makes it possible. In bringing home what it feels like to be a refugee, *Exit West* makes ethical and political claims upon the reader. "The novel asks readers why doors should be closed to refugees when the readers of the novel might become refugees one day."[60]

Online comments include examples of readers engaging seriously with these concerns. An Amazon reviewer, for example, writes that "*Exit West* challenges you to think in new ways about a familiar issue, to question what you understand when you see generic terms like refugee or migrant applied to millions of individuals, who each has their home, their emotional life, their door, and has to make the decision to take that chance, or not, while they can."[61] This observation gets to the heart of the novel's choices: its turn away from exoticism and sensationalism; its emphasis on emotional and existential, as well as political, dilemmas; its portrayal of migration as a shared experience, albeit one inflected in very different ways. Nguyen's own review adopts a similar tactic: buttonholing its readers, putting them in the position of refugees, and emphasizing the ordinariness of a way of life:

> You wake in the morning and drink your coffee or tea. You drive a car or a motorbike, or perhaps you take the bus. You go to work and turn on your computer. You go out at night and flirt and date. . . . [Y]ou keep believing you are human even when the catastrophe arrives and renders you homeless. Your town or city or countryside is in ruins. You try to make it to the border. Only then, hoping to leave, or making it across the border, do you understand that those who live on the other side do not see you as human at all.[62]

Whether such attempts to create empathy will result in changes in action or long-term behavior remains, of course, an open question. But we should look askance at the expectation that a novel should trigger some kind of radical change—and that if it fails to do so, it must therefore be mired in ideological complicity. "That people may feel empathy or sympathy without becoming political actors," Kim Chabot Davis remarks in her study of cross-racial identification, "is not a fault inherent in the emotions."[63] Davis goes on: "many other individual circumstances—political ideologies, an ability to be self-critical, witnessing of discrimination, previous encounters

with people of color, other cross-cultural encounters, and in-
nate variations in empathic ability—all play a role in making
empathetic responses possible."[64] Change can only be a result
of many things coming together—not of a single, all-powerful
agent acting alone.

There are, as we have now come to see, different ways of
getting close to characters, though these strands are often intertwined in various combinations. In *Jane Eyre*, for example,
there is a formal *alignment* with the heroine's first-person perspective; the novel orients readers toward *allegiance* with Jane
as the novel's moral center; it invites female readers to *recognize*
gender-based barriers they have also encountered; finally, it
encourages *empathy* by dwelling on the heroine's impassioned
responses to hardship and misrecognition. Thanks to this thick
rope of connection, Brontë's novel has been highly effective in
promoting identification. Yet here again, there are certainly no
guarantees. In Michelle Cliff's *No Telephone to Heaven*, for example, the heroine struggles against identifying in a manner
that has been echoed by numerous postcolonial critics: "The fiction had tricked her. Drawn her in so that she became Jane. . . .
With a sharpness of mind, she reprimanded herself. No, she told
herself, she could not be Jane."[65] Since Brontë's novel is part of
a colonial education and since the Caribbean heroine of Cliff's
novel has acquired an anticolonial consciousness, any sense of
commonality can feel only like a fraught capitulation. The ties
between Brontë's protagonist and female readers have considerable durability and strength; but there is nothing inevitable
about them.

The affordances of other texts, meanwhile, may pan out
quite differently. In the Sherlock Holmes stories, we are *aligned*
with Watson's perspective; but any allegiance is likely to be to
Holmes. First-person narration often encourages identification
with the narrator—but not when he is utterly subordinate to
his charismatic companion. Who cares about, dreams about,
wants to be Watson? Meanwhile, in reading an Ian Fleming

novel, we are formally aligned with Bond and also invited to root for him (an allegiance that need not reflect any real-world commitments—caught up in *Goldfinger*, I feel a flicker of delight as Bond outwits his villainous opponent, even though I have no interest in saving the free world from Soviet conspiracies). But what about empathy? As Umberto Eco pointed out decades ago, 007 is a magnificent machine who lacks interiority and is voided of any complex emotions. Similar issues arise in the very different literary world of Camus's *The Stranger*; Meursault's famous opening lines on his mother's death advertise his lack of empathy and are likely to block the reader's own. There are notable parallels, in this respect, between action-driven genre fiction and some canonical works of modernist literature: a shared, often strenuous avoidance of co-feeling (though readers may experience a form of "kinesthetic empathy" that is anchored in bodily sensations rather than emotional depth, such as sensing the harsh assault of the blazing sun with Meursault and flinching with Bond as he receives a hard kick in the ribs from Goldfinger).

We are now in a position to question the frequent conflation of identification with empathy—as if the former always implied or required the latter. In her very useful book on empathy, for example, Suzanne Keen frequently switches between the two terms in claiming that audiences are primed to identify even with cartoon or fairy-tale characters: Little Red Riding Hood, Garfield, or Charlie Brown.[66] While endorsing the overall point, I'd argue that attachment to such schematic figures has far more to do with alignment, allegiance, and recognition than with empathy—which *is* tied to interiority and the sympathetic rendering of emotional states. This distinction also explains the pushback from critics against attempts to make empathy a catchall term for justifying the value of literature. Such a word—with its connotations of concern, fellow feeling, and altruism—seems exceptionally ill-suited to the demented, destructive, antinomian, and asocial heroes of much modern and postmodern fiction, from *Notes from Underground* to *American Psycho*. These figures are often fascinating, without a doubt—but their draw has little to do with empathy.

I should perhaps clarify that I am not "against empathy," which strikes me as a fundament of pro-social interaction and the public good. Attempts to pitch empathy as the main form of aesthetic engagement, however, quickly fall afoul of numerous counterexamples. Let us look at a few such counterexamples in more detail. Our baseline definition still holds—identification implies a sense of something shared; it often relies on person schemas—but we are now conscious of the differing ways in which this relation can unfold. And we can take on board what might seem like a counterintuitive claim: that the readings carried out by literary scholars—however erudite, ironic, skeptical, or critical—are not "outside" identification but premised upon it.

IRONIC IDENTIFICATION

In a recent book on the writing of *The Stranger*, Alice Kaplan ponders the paradoxical draw of its protagonist. How, she wonders, can indifference be so fascinating? (The original reader's report for French publisher Gallimard referred to Meursault as "inhuman" in his indifference.) Camus fashioned a character who is incapable of empathy—and who seems, in turn, to inspire little or no empathy in readers. And yet the fascination exerted by *The Stranger* is incontrovertible. "How," Kaplan writes, "can such a distant and empty narrator capture so much attention, and how can a disturbing book elicit so much loyalty?"[67] Peeling identification away from empathy makes such attachment much less puzzling than it would otherwise be.

Beyond alignment—the novel's centering on the thoughts and sensations of Meursault—allegiance and recognition offer themselves as relevant concepts in clarifying the allure of *The Stranger*. But what kind of allegiance? And what is being recognized? Allegiance might seem an odd word for a character who seems so asocial and disengaged. How can readers ally themselves with someone so impervious to any bid for connection? Any sense of recognition, meanwhile, is likely to be partial and qualified, not a point-by-point matching but rather a sense that Camus's hero captures aspects of a reader's sense of being in the world.

In introducing the idea of ironic identification, I do not mean the same thing as Hans-Robert Jauss: that identifying can be interrupted or broken by moments of ironic distancing.[68] Rather, I want to highlight a style of response that has received virtually no attention: an identification that is *premised or based on irony.* That is to say, a sense of estrangement and disassociation is the connecting tissue binding character and reader. What is held in common is an experience of having nothing in common with others, of feeling at odds with the mainstream of social life. Quite a few protagonists of modern fiction—solitary, adrift, and sardonic or melancholic—solicit such forms of affiliation: *The Immoralist, Nausea, Invisible Man, The Piano Teacher.* And here the vectors of causality are hard to pin down. Are readers drawn to fictional figures who crystallize their own feelings of anomie, or are they schooled in a sense of estrangement and ennui by reading works of modernist literature? The result, in either case, is what we might call an alliance of strangers: fictional and real persons linked by a shared sense of disassociation. It is often assumed that identifying and irony are mutually exclusive: where one is, the other cannot be. And yet irony turns out to be a surprisingly common means of identification.

We see such a tie in both academic and popular responses to Camus's novel. A lay reader remarks of Meursault: "he wasn't a character meant to sympathize with, or relate to. He wasn't even much of a character until the last chapter. He was a montage of existentialism: an indifferent symbol robotic in attitude. . . . What *The Stranger* said about God and what little time we have to dwell on such uncertainties is beautiful. And I completely agree."[69] Acknowledging the irrelevance of an empathic bond, this reader allies himself with Meursault's railing against religion; he points to philosophical themes ("montage of existentialism") rather than psychological affinities. Here again, we see how ideas serve as mediators between works and readers. Such a response, of course, is prompted not just by the novel but by its framing; *The Stranger* is often encountered in the classroom, paired with explications of theories of the absurd. And yet this is not at all to imply that philosophical themes cannot have affective force. In a memorable anecdote, the British philosopher R. M. Hare captures the effect of Camus's novel on his young Swiss houseguest, whose behavior and attitudes changed markedly after reading *The Stranger* and becoming persuaded that "nothing matters." He took up smoking, skulked in his bedroom, was taciturn at dinner, and went for long, aimless walks around the outskirts of Oxford. There was no doubt at all, Hare remarks, "about the violence with which he had been affected by what he had read."[70]

Meanwhile, *The Stranger* is not a "novel of ideas" in the usual sense: the absurd, for Camus, has far more to do with sensation than with thought. Neither subjective (housed in the mind) nor objective (a systematic philosophy), it is a nose-to-nose encounter with the sheer senselessness of phenomena. And here, for some readers, a sense of recognition comes into play: as being less a matter of what is said than *how* it is said. Reflecting on his early fascination with *The Stranger*, novelist Aaron Gwyn writes: "It was the voice I connected with first, antihero Meursault's poker-faced assessment of a world that makes as little sense to him as mine did to me." The language of voice becomes a way of mediating style through character, though without conflating the two. An affinity is registered; Meursault's flatness of tone resonates with his own sense of disassociation; there is a common condition of being unmoored, out of sync with one's milieu. And yet identification is partial, not total: "It was comforting to consider the ways the two of us were alike, more comforting to consider all the ways we were different."[71] Along similar lines, Neal Oxenhandler speaks of a negative identification: what connects him to Meursault—along an axis of recognition—is a shared lack of affect, a common inability to feel the appropriate, socially sanctioned emotions.[72]

Is the draw of Camus's protagonist—detached, distant, emotionally avoidant—limited to male readers? Some commentators have suggested as much. "If one reads as a woman or as an Arab," one critic remarks, ". . . one's tendency to identify with Meursault or to cast him in a sympathetic light will thereby be reduced if not altogether stifled."[73] Yet experiences of estrangement or disassociation are hardly limited to white men. In a fascinating book, for example, Deborah Nelson captures the ethos of unsentimentality—being tough, impersonal, nonempathic, even coldhearted—that defined a cohort of midcentury female intellectuals, including Mary McCarthy, Hannah Arendt, Susan Sontag, and Simone Weil.[74] Meanwhile, the publication of Kamel Daoud's *The Meursault Investigation* pulverizes any generalities about reading "as an Arab." Told from the viewpoint of Harun, the imagined brother of the man murdered by Meursault, the novel is a sustained reckoning with the racial politics of literary alignment. It reflects at length on how *The Stranger* erases, in its indifference, the name and the personhood of the dead Arab, and how this erasure is conveyed to and registered by the work's readers.

Yet the novel is also an extended homage to Camus's work, in its laconic and pared-back prose as well as in its narrative technique. The narrator seeks exculpation for his own murderous act by recounting his story to a stranger in a bar, in a manner reminiscent of another work by Camus, *The Fall*. And like *The Fall*, Daoud's novel is a brilliant exercise in unreliable narration: Harun's evasions and silences become increasingly evident, troubling the sense of solidarity that the novel solicits. The reader is bound to the main character, yet also estranged from him.[75] And the work concludes with a fierce blast of recognition:

a tie between Harun and Meursault, an acknowledgment of similarity across no-less-real racial and cultural differences. "I was looking for traces of my brother in the book," writes Harun of *The Stranger*, "and what I found there instead was my own reflection, I discovered I was practically the murderer's double."[76]

The import of ironic identification, moreover, reaches well beyond *The Stranger* and other works of literary modernism into the intellectual culture and ethos of the present-day humanities—as one of the main ways in which critical personae are formed and alliances are created. Camus's existential irony differs philosophically from the poststructuralist irony that succeeded it, yet there are notable similarities at the level of sensibility and disposition. Lee Konstantinou summarizes the present-day variant in his survey of contemporary criticism: "the ironist debunks rigid ideologies, unweaves foundationalist 'master narratives' and deconstructs every conceptual or philosophical description of the world through the close investigation of language. To be an ironist is to have the power and inclination to reveal the gaps and holes in hegemonic conceptions that pass themselves off as common sense."[77] Such an ethos of disassociation serves—paradoxically—as a form of glue, binding critics to other like-minded critics as well as to works of art that are held to embrace a similar skepticism toward the commonsensical and commonplace. It is via the presumption of shared estrangement that intellectual, interpersonal, and institutional ties are forged.

Faye Halpern traces out such bonds as they are manifested in American studies, looking closely at the history of commentaries on *Benito Cereno* and *Uncle Tom's Cabin*. Stowe's novel is often censured for inspiring identification and emotional or sentimental responses that gloss over the structural realities of slavery. *Benito Cereno*, by contrast, is widely admired as a self-undermining text that leaves few footholds for interpretation. Deploying irony as both a trope and a structural device, it seems to thwart any desire for attachment. And yet, as Halpern points out, critical testimonies to these ironic or self-qualifying aspects of Melville's text reveal ample evidence of identification on the part of critics: with *Benito Cereno*, with Melville, with what they perceive as the work's subversive aims.[78] In short, while identification-as-empathy may attract censure from American studies scholars, other kinds of attachments are very much in force. Recognizing traces of her own intellectual or political commitments in the work she is reading, the critic allies herself with its techniques of estrangement and critical distancing.

Similar instances of ironic identification can be found in other fields in the humanities. An essay in the journal *Feminist Theory*, for example, offers a rereading of *The Story of O*, arguing that O's embrace of her sexual objectification serves as a critical commentary on women's lack of agency. "What the text reveals . . . is the ambiguity of femininity in the modern era and the difficulties that arise from that constraint."[79] The critic discovers in Réage's novel a protofeminist perspective that is akin to her own: that is, she *recognizes* a shared stance of dissent. This recognition in turn inspires a sense of *allegiance* with *The Story of O* and against another portrayal of female masochism, *Fifty Shades of Grey*; the latter is taken to task for serving up a regressive romantic fantasy and purveying a neoliberal vision of sexuality. As in Halpern's example, the issue is not one of identification versus its absence but of the value allotted to different *kinds* of identification: empathy versus recognition and allegiance; ties to fictional persons versus ties to a critical, subversive, or ironic stance that is attributed to the overall "project" of a text.

It's worth pointing out, moreover, that person schemas do not vanish from even the most ardently antihumanist styles of scholarship—shaping relations to other scholars if not to fictional figures. Scholars may profess skepticism about the status of characters, yet they cannot entirely circumvent the matrix of character. Irony is a matter of embracing a certain ethos: not only a way of reading but also a sensibility, disposition, and style. And here certain thinkers and theorists come to assume exemplary importance and are endowed with a surplus of charismatic authority. Influential figures—Lacan, Derrida,

Foucault, Spivak, Butler, Fish—have inspired identification among critics, David Shumway observes, in much the same way as stars of the studio era once commanded the identification of movie audiences.[80] Such writers serve as objects of affective, as well as intellectual, investments; critics cathect not only onto ideas but also onto an imagined persona behind these ideas and the attitudes, sensibilities, and ways of being in the world that he or she is held to embody.

CONCLUSION

Acts of identifying, I've argued, drive various kinds of engagement with fiction. Connections are forged across differences; expected or surprising affinities come to light; ties are created that may be self-transformative or that eddy out into larger social currents. Such ties often involve empathy—and yet it is not uncommon to identify with fictional figures who block empathy rather than foster it. It is here that ties of recognition and allegiance prove more pertinent—keeping in mind that these ties may be ambivalent, qualified, partial, or ironic.

I've also questioned certain beliefs about character—for example, that it denotes an emotionally complex, well-rounded, deep, yet unified personage. This view coincides with the stress on empathy and the dominance of realist examples in many literary-critical accounts of character. How many theses about character—whether positive or critical—have been built on a handful of novels by Dickens, Eliot, and James! To grapple with character in its richness and variety, the net must be cast more broadly. This means factoring in popular genres, where character may function rather differently: that James Bond is a "man without qualities," as Kingsley Amis points out, serves to facilitate identification rather than to block it.[81] Meanwhile, that figures in modernist literature differ—formally, thematically, philosophically—from those of nineteenth-century novels does not mean they no longer "count" as characters. Some of the most memorable figures of fiction include Clarissa Dalloway,

Leopold Bloom, Mrs. Ramsay, Joseph K, Mother Courage, the duchesse de Guermantes, Gregor Samsa; whether they are felt to be round or flat is beside the point.[82]

Divisions between a specialized guild of interpreters who are concerned with knowledge and meaning and a lay audience that is driven by feeling and pleasure, remarks Deidre Lynch, result in a very partial picture of both.[83] I have queried one aspect of this dichotomy by taking another look at identification. It is not that naive readers or viewers identify while dispassionate critics withhold attachment; rather, they find different points of connection—affective, ethical, political, philosophical, or some mix of all these. Meanwhile, ties to fictional beings are formed in a wide variety of genres, from the hermetic to the formulaic. These fictional beings are Janus-faced figures who point to real persons and their own fabricated status. They have their own reality, force, and weight of being. Let's give these characters their due.

NOTES

The writing of this chapter was supported by a grant from the Danish National Research Foundation: DNRF 127. A very early version of the argument about identification—though not character—was sketched out in "Identification and Critique," in *Projecting American Studies: Essays on Theory, Method, and Practice*, ed. Frank Kelleter and Alexander Starre (Heidelberg: Winter, 2018). I would like to thank Elaine Auyoung, Carl Plantinga, and Ika Willis for their helpful comments on the chapter, Jon Najarian for his response at the PAL workshop at Duke University in March 2018, Amanda Anderson and Toril Moi for productive conversations, and my "Uses of Literature" colleagues at the University of Southern Denmark for their perceptive insights.

1. Faye Halpern, "In Defense of Reading Badly: The Politics of Identification in *Benito Cereno, Uncle Tom's Cabin*, and Our Classrooms," *College English* 70, no. 6 (2008): 56.

2. For activation and motivation as defining features of character, see the introduction to *Characters in Fictional Worlds*, ed. Jens Eder, Fotis Annidis, and Ralf Schneider (Berlin: De Gruyter, 2010), 10.

3. Susan Sontag, "Notes on 'Camp,'" in *Against Interpretation and Other Essays* (New York: Picador, 2001), 286.

4. A generalization, admittedly, though not an inaccurate one. I should emphasize, however, that I have found the ideas of some film scholars working under the general rubric of cognitive psychology very helpful, especially the work of Murray Smith and Carl Plantinga.

5. Jackie Stacey, *Stargazing: Hollywood Cinema and Female Spectatorship* (London: Routledge, 1994), 126.

6. The phrase "Vulcan mindmeld"—often cited in accounts of identification by analytical philosophers—comes from Noel Carroll, *The Philosophy of Horror; or, Paradoxes of the Heart* (New York: Routledge, 1990), 89.

7. Ien Ang, *Watching "Dallas": Soap Opera and the Melodramatic Imagination* (London: Routledge 1985); Janice Radway, *Reading the Romance: Women, Patriarchy, and Popular Literature* (Durham: University of North Carolina Press, 1991); Janice Radway, *A Feeling for Books: The Book-of-the-Month Club, Literary Taste, and Middle-Class Desire* (Durham: University of North Carolina Press, 1999); Stacey, *Stargazing*; Judith Mayne, *Cinema and Spectatorship* (London: Routledge, 1993).

8. Douglas Crimp, "Right on Girlfriend!," in *Fear of a Queer Planet: Queer Politics and Social Theory* (Minneapolis: University of Minnesota Press, 1993), 316; Diana Fuss, *Identification Papers: Readings on Psychoanalysis, Sexuality, and Culture* (New York: Routledge, 1995), 8.

9. All quotations are from Michael Montlack, ed., *My Diva: 65 Gay Men on the Women Who Inspire Them* (Madison, WI: Terrace Books, 2009). See, respectively, 140, 24, 46, 23.

10. For a good discussion of this issue, see Marco Carraciolo, *Strange Narrators in Contemporary Fiction: Explorations in Read-*

ers' Engagements with Character (Lincoln: University of Nebraska Press, 2016).

11. Jeanette Winterson, *Why Be Happy When You Could Be Normal?* (London: Grove Press, 2013), 117.

12. *Ibid.*, 61.

13. *Ibid.*, 220.

14. See Rita Felski, *"Hooked: Art and Attachment"* (unpublished book manuscript).

15. Blakey Vermeule, *Why Do We Care about Literary Characters?* (Baltimore: Johns Hopkins University Press, 2011).

16. Or perhaps I am speaking only of myself here.

17. Mario Vargas Llosa, *The Perpetual Orgy: Flaubert and Madame Bovary* (New York: Farrar, Straus and Giroux, 1987), 7. For an account of reader fascination with immoral or unpleasant characters, see Katherine Tullmann, "Sympathy and Fascination," *British Journal of Aesthetics* 56, no. 2 (2016):115–29.

18. Vargas Llosa, *Perpetual Orgy*, 13.

19. Bruno Latour, *An Inquiry into Modes of Existence* (Cambridge, MA: Harvard University Press, 2014), 13.

20. Jeremy Rosen, *Minor Characters Have Their Day: Genre and the Contemporary Literary Marketplace* (New York: Columbia University Press, 2016).

21. Francesca Coppa, *The Fanfiction Reader: Folk Tales for the Digital Age* (Ann Arbor: University of Michigan Press, 2017), 13.

22. [Daniel] Mallory Ortberg, *Texts from Jane Eyre and Other Conversations with Your Favorite Literary Characters* (New York: Henry Holt, 2004).

23. For a helpful discussion of *Umwelt*, see Riin Magnus and Kalevi Kull, "Roots of Culture in the Umwelt," in *The Oxford Handbook of Culture and Psychology*, ed. Jaan Valsiner (Oxford: Oxford University Press, 2012), 649–66.

24. See Jon Helt Haarder, "A Story We Are Part Of: Introducing Performative Biographism by Way of Reading Karl Ove Knausgaard's *My Struggle* (and Vice Versa)," in *Expectations: Reader Assumptions and Author Intentions in Narrative Discourse*, ed. Stine

Slot Grumsen et al. (Copenhagen: Medusa, 2017), 118–43; and also Toril Moi, "Describing *My Struggle*," *The Point*, December 27, 2017, https://thepointmag.com/2017/criticism/describing-my-struggle -knausgaard.

25. Stacey, *Stargazing*, 146.

26. Erwin Panofsky, "Style and Medium in the Motion Pictures," in *Film: An Anthology*, ed. Daniel Talbot (1959; Berkeley: University of California Press, 1970), 29.

27. Richard Dyer, *Stars* (London: British Film Institute, 1979), 178.

28. Hélène Mialet, *Hawking Incorporated: Stephen Hawking and the Anthropology of the Knowing Subject* (Chicago: University of Chicago Press, 2012).

29. Jon Najarian, "Response to Rita Felski, 'Identifying with Characters,'" paper presented at PAL workshop, Duke University, March 2018.

30. https://www.theguardian.com/books/2017/feb/14/fictional -characters-make-existential-crossings-into-real-life-study-finds.

31. Latour, *Inquiry*, 242.

32. T. W. Adorno, "The Position of the Narrator in the Contemporary Novel," in *Notes to Literature*, vol. 1, trans. Shierry Weber Nicholsen (New York: Columbia University Press, 1991), 30–36.

33. Julian Murphet, "The Mole and the Multiple: A Chiasmus of Character," *New Literary History* 42, no. 2 (2011): 255–76.

34. Hans-Robert Jauss, *Aesthetic Experience and Literary Hermeneutics*, trans. Michael Shaw (Minneapolis: University of Minnesota Press, 1982), xxix.

35. See Murray Smith, "On the Twofoldedness of Character," *New Literary History* 42, no. 2 (2011): 277–94.

36. Rebecca Solnit, "Men Explain *Lolita* to Me," https://lithub .com/men-explain-lolita-to-me/.

37. Murray Smith, *Engaging Characters: Fiction, Emotion, and the Cinema* (Oxford: Clarendon Press, 1995). My differences from Smith can be summarized as follows: I retain the term "identification," which he rejects in favor of a (in my view, overly broad) notion of engagement; he devotes a chapter to recognition as a

perceptual matter but does not address its phenomenological or sociological aspects; he draws a strong distinction between empathy and sympathy, whereas I see the differences between these two terms as much less significant. Nonetheless, I have found Smith's overall approach very helpful.

38. Emily Nussbaum, "The Great Divide: Norman Lear, Archie Bunker, and the Rise of the Bad Fan," *New Yorker*, April 7, 2014, 64–68. For an account of a reader identifying with Casaubon, see Suzanne Keen, *Empathy and the Novel* (Oxford: Oxford University Press, 2007), 75. Scholars in cultural studies have written at great length about audiences reading against the grain of conservative texts, but little attention has been paid to the opposite scenario: conservative readings of progressive works.

39. Steven Connor, *Theory and Cultural Value* (Oxford: Blackwell, 1992).

40. Carl Plantinga, *Screen Stories: Emotion and the Ethics of Engagement* (Oxford: Oxford University Press, 2018).

41. On the links between aesthetic and political representation as they play out in the field of literary studies, see John Guillory, *Cultural Capital: The Problem of Literary Canon Formation* (Chicago: University of Chicago Press, 1993).

42. See Rita Felski, *Beyond Feminist Aesthetics: Feminist Literature and Social Change* (Cambridge, MA: Harvard University Press, 1989).

43. Sheila Benson, "Thelma & Louise Just Good Ol' Boys?," *Los Angeles Times*, May 31, 1991; Margaret Carlson, "Is This What Feminism Is All About?," *Time*, June 24, 1991.

44. Bernie Cook, ed., *Thelma and Louise Live! The Cultural Afterlife of an American Film* (Austin: University of Texas Press, 2007), 34.

45. Kim Chabot Davis, *Postmodern Texts and Emotional Audiences* (West Lafayette, IN: Purdue University Press, 2007), 65.

46. For an account of the many obstacles that had to be overcome before the film could be made, see Becky Aikman, *Off the Cliff: How the Making of Thelma and Louise Drove Hollywood to the Edge* (New York: Penguin, 2017).

47. Interview with Callie Khouri, in Cook, *Thelma and Louise Live!*, 184. On limited views of identification in debates about the film, see Sharon Willis, "Hardware and Hardbodies, What Do Women Want? A Reading of *Thelma and Louise*," in *Film Theory Goes to the Movies: Cultural Analysis of Contemporary Films*, ed. Jim Collins et al. (New York: Routledge, 2012), 120–28.

48. Paul Ricoeur, *Time and Narrative*, vol. 1, trans. Kathleen McLaughlin and David Pellauer (Chicago: University of Chicago Press, 1984), 59. Dorothy J. Hale argues that poststructuralist critics who profess their distrust of ethical norms are nonetheless bestowing an ethical content on radical otherness. Dorothy J. Hale, "Fiction as Restriction: Self-Binding in New Ethical Theories of the Novel," *Narrative* 15, no. 2 (2007): 187–206; Dorothy J. Hale, "Aesthetics and the New Ethics: Theorizing the Novel in the Twenty-First Century," *PMLA* 124, no. 3 (2009): 896–905.

49. Rita Felski, *Uses of Literature* (Oxford: Blackwell, 2008), 25.

50. Robert Cohen, "'The Piano Has Been Drinking': The Art of the Rant," *Georgia Review* 59, no. 2 (2005): 234.

51. Thomas Bernhard, *The Loser*, trans. Jack Dawson (New York: Vintage, 1991), 38.

52. Gary Indiana, "Saint Bernhard: Preface to a Multi-volume Suicide Note," *Village Voice Literary Supplement*, March 5, 1996.

53. Ethan Reed, "Forms of Frustration: Unrest and Unfulfillment in American Literature after 1934" (PhD diss., University of Virginia, 2019).

54. For a helpful overview of the relevant debates, see the introduction to *Empathy: Philosophical and Psychological Perspectives*, ed. Amy Coplan and Peter Goldie (Oxford: Oxford University Press, 2017).

55. Ann Jurecic, "Empathy and the Critic," *College English* 74, no. 1 (2011): 10.

56. Jurecic, "Empathy and the Critic," 279.

57. Kiley Garrett was an undergraduate student in my Theories of Reading class at the University of Virginia in the spring of 2017. This sentence is drawn from her essay on empathy.

58. Mohsin Hamid, *Exit West: A Novel* (New York: Riverhead Books, 2017), 4.

59. Ibid., 167.

60. Viet Thanh Nguyen, "A Refugee Crisis in a World of Open Doors," *New York Times*, March 10, 2017.

61. Kate Vane, amazon.com, March 2, 2017.

62. Nguyen, "Refugee Crisis."

63. Kim Chabot Davis, *Beyond the White Negro: Empathy and Anti-racist Reading* (Urbana: University of Illinois Press, 2014), 12.

64. *Ibid.*, 13.

65. Michelle Cliff, *No Telephone to Heaven* (New York: Plume, 1996), 116.

66. Keen, *Empathy and the Novel*.

67. Alice Kaplan, *Looking for "The Stranger": Albert Camus and the Life of a Literary Classic* (Chicago: University of Chicago Press, 2016), 2.

68. Jauss, *Aesthetic Experience and Literary Hermeneutics*, 181–88.

69. Joanna Gavins, *Reading the Absurd* (Edinburgh: Edinburgh University Press, 2013), 28.

70. R. M. Hare, "Nothing Matters," in *Applications of Moral Philosophy* (London: Macmillan, 1972), 105. I am grateful to John Kulka for pointing me to this example.

71. Aaron Gwyn, http://www.npr.org/2014/08/10/336823512 /albert-camus-poker-faced-stranger-became-a-much-needed -friend.

72. Neal Oxenhandler, *Looking for Heroes in Postwar France: Albert Camus, Max Jacob, Simone Weil* (Hanover, NH: University Press of New England, 1996), 20.

73. English Showalter Jr., *"The Stranger": Humanity and the Absurd* (Boston: Twayne, 1989), 17.

74. Deborah Nelson, *Tough Enough: Arbus, Arendt, Didion, McCarthy, Sontag, Weil* (Chicago: University of Chicago Press, 2017).

75. For a detailed analysis of this dynamic, see James Phelan, "Estranging Unreliability, Bonding Unreliability, and the Ethics of *Lolita*," *Narrative* 15, no. 2 (2007): 222–38.

76. Kamel Daoud, *The Meursault Investigation* (New York: Other Press, 2015), 131.

77. Lee Konstantinou, *Cool Characters: Irony and American Fiction* (Cambridge, MA: Harvard University Press, 2016), 31.

78. Halpern, "In Defense of Reading Badly."

79. Amber Jamilla Musser, "BDSM and the Boundaries of Criticism: Feminism and Neoliberalism in *Fifty Shades of Grey* and *The Story of O*," *Feminist Theory* 16, no. 2 (2015): 126.

80. David Shumway, "Disciplinary Identities," in *Affiliations: Identity in Academic Culture*, ed. Jeffrey di Leo (Lincoln: University of Nebraska Press, 2003), 93. On the relations between irony, character, and the ethos of criticism, see Amanda Anderson, *The Way We Argue Now: A Study in the Cultures of Theory* (Princeton, NJ: Princeton University Press, 2006).

81. Kingsley Amis, *The James Bond Dossier* (London: Jonathan Cape, 1965), 43.

82. For recent, if rather different, defenses of flat characters, see James Wood, *How Fiction Works* (New York: Farrar, Straus and Giroux, 2008); Marta Figlerowicz, *Flat Protagonists: A Theory of Novel Character* (Oxford: Oxford University Press, 2016).

83. Deidre Lynch, *Loving Literature* (Chicago: University of Chicago Press, 2015), 12.

THINKING WITH CHARACTER

Amanda Anderson

"In or about December, 1910, human character changed."[1] This statement by Virginia Woolf from "Mr. Bennett and Mrs. Brown" is widely known and cited by literary scholars. Housed as it is within an essay of literary history, the assertion plays on the dual meaning of character as both a literary and a moral concept, inviting consideration of the historical conditions of literary form as well as the ways social and political forces alter how individuals and classes of people are seen and represented. Woolf's own observations about social and literary history in "Mr. Bennett and Mrs. Brown" are ultimately in the service of a conception of individual character that retains its ineluctable particularity, and a conception of the writer as one who ideally manages to convey and promote the idea "that there is something permanently interesting in character in itself."[2] As it proceeds, the essay develops into an attack on the overattention to sociological detail in the writings of the Edwardians as compared to those "great novelists"—Tolstoy, Thackeray, Sterne, Flaubert, Austen, Hardy, Charlotte Brontë—who "have brought us to see whatever they wish us to see through some character." "Otherwise," continues Woolf, "they would not be novelists; but poets, historians, pamphleteers."[3]

What tends to go unremarked about Woolf's famous and playfully gnomic statement is that it is the "second assertion" in the short paragraph in which it appears. The full paragraph reads:

My first assertion is one that I think you will grant—that everyone in this room is a judge of character. Indeed it would be impossible to live for a year without disaster unless one practiced character-reading and had some skill in the art. Our marriages, our friendships depend on it; our business largely depends on it; every day questions arise which can only be solved by its help. And I will hazard a second assertion, which is more disputable perhaps, to the effect that in or about December, 1910, human character changed.[4]

Certain things are notable about Woolf's first assertion as well as the overall effect of the two statements as the launching claims of the essay. First, Woolf works easily with a conception of character understood as a natural focus for the writer, and in a way that does not imagine any problematic gap between character in life and character as it is realized on the page. In this sense we could say that her conception of character carries with it a realist assumption and a realist standard, acknowledging the difficulty of capturing character but taking for granted that readers expect to see character represented through the craft of the writer. For Woolf, part of what engages both writers and readers is a fundamental and everyday interest in people and the characters they present. Second, there is an understated yet absolutely basic emphasis on the centrality of moral character to human relations. Given the stakes—averting disaster in the case of one's most intimate or vital relations—judging character perhaps means knowing whether or to what extent someone is reliable or true; whether or in what way they possess a certain integrity; whether and to what extent they can be counted on.[5]

There is no sense, in light of the embellished anecdote about Mrs. Brown and of the novels of Woolf herself, that such judgments are or need be blunt or reductive—it is not a simple matter of whether a person is good or not. In the case of Woolf's Mrs. Brown, whom she encounters as a fellow passenger in a railway carriage, the most salient inferences drawn from her "pinched" look include suffering, apprehension, and want: "I felt that she had nobody to support her; that she had to make up her mind for herself; that, having been deserted, or left a widow, years ago, she had led an anxious, harried life, bringing up an only son, perhaps, who as likely as not, was by this time beginning to go to the bad."[6] Without disregarding the significant social markers so important to the novelists she criticizes, Woolf gives centrality to the tragic elements of Mrs. Brown's private life, as well as their extension across time and into the next generation. In imagining Mrs. Brown's relation to her male companion on the train, moreover, Woolf expands on the legible ways in which Mrs. Brown appears to be at his mercy with regard to some harassing matter, perhaps legal in nature. While Mrs. Brown's character is socially situated, it compels us in part through the manner in which it confronts or endures challenging experiences of grief or loss. Indeed, understanding character within the larger context of a life and over time is of supreme importance for Woolf, and such understanding simultaneously involves social, psychological, and moral assessment.

CHARACTER AND THE MORAL LIFE: DISCIPLINARY CONTEXTS

It is often assumed that within the last couple of decades literary critics have begun a salutary turn to character after a long period in which other forms of analysis made the discussion of character, whether in formal or in substantial terms, unlikely or difficult. Associations of character criticism with the elevation of the individual subject or the investments of humanism were among the key contributors to character's occluded place in much literary criticism. Still, there remained throughout the period from the 1980s through the turn of the century an interest in the representation of subjectivity and of individuals defined sociologically (by gender, race, class, ethnicity, or sexuality), which inevitably involved a focus on characters as bearers of these identities. For example, Foucauldian approaches explored the constitution of the private subject or forms of interiority within the rise of disciplinary society; and queer studies explored stances of antinormativity and scenarios of desire between subjects, which involved discussion of literary characters along with forms of narration or plot itineraries. These are simply two examples among many. What seems to have come to the fore in the newer character criticism, by contrast, is the exploration of how we understand and relate to literary characters. It is an approach that is at once more avowedly formalist and at the same time engaged with the moral, epistemological, and phenomenological questions associated with representing people and with reading texts that include such representations. A catalyzing work for these discussions was Alex Woloch's *The One vs. the Many* (2003), which aimed to mediate between humanist and structuralist models by introducing the concept of the character-system and by focusing on the minor character. A decade later John Frow's *Character and Person* (2014) also directly addressed the challenge of understanding literary characters as both formal representations and "person-like objects," arguing that we must acknowledge literary characters as "ontologically hybrid." Also relevant to this phenomenon was Blakey Vermeule's *Why Do We Care about Literary Characters?* (2010), which used a sociohistorically inflected evolutionary psychology approach to explain how and why we are interested in characters.[7]

I am not convinced, however, that these approaches really capture the kind of interest in character that Woolf describes and that I will argue is critical to an understanding of how novels uniquely present forms of moral experience. Turning one's attention to character may disclose many things. It may help one to understand the novelist's view of social hierarchy or gender or class, or other forms of selfhood variously situated. It may reveal how the novelist construes villainy and heroism and the many shades of gray between the two. But character also helps writers present forms of inner experience that are extremely difficult to capture in other media or in the academic genres of

the human sciences. One such experience is interior moral reflection as it extends across time. The novel has a special capacity and license to convey the phenomenology of the thinking
life, and it has demonstrated a special interest in forms of thinking since its inception. One of the greatest formal achievements
of the novel is its refined capacity to present interior monologue
through free indirect discourse and, more broadly, its ability to
use point of view and narrative voice to mediate between the
discourse of the narrator and the discourse of the characters.[8]
And yet, curiously, there has been little attention paid to dis-
tinctively moral forms of ongoing reflection in the novel and
virtually no focus on a species of thinking I will designate as rumination. I hope in this essay to draw attention to this concept
and this mode of thinking, so as to open out new ways of exploring how we understand the moral life of literary characters.

As long as a focus on character tells us something about
the ways in which individuality is an ideological fiction or how
identity is constituted through textual forms or fields of power,
it does not fundamentally disrupt the prevailing paradigms of
literary criticism installed in the last decades of the previous
century. Character criticism allied to questions of the moral
life, by contrast, is seen as problematically tied to an outmoded
humanism. Frow's own discussion of what he calls "ethical criticism" is symptomatic. He first identifies two different "faces"
of ethical criticism, one which "involves the widespread use of
the notion of 'story' or 'narrative' to define the formation and
coherence of the self" and another as "the liberal doctrine of
the freely self-governing and self-shaping individual, with its
positing of a direct continuity between moral and literary character." He then goes on to assert that the latter approach essen-
tially underwrites a problematic pedagogy, advanced through
"moral analysis," which allows for the promotion of moral education through a treatment of the literary character as unified
and "real" and which fails to grasp conditions of "textuality."
Beyond this, Frow argues that ethical criticism more generally

promotes a certain "mysticism of the self which is characteristic of humanist theory."[9]

Despite the seeming evenhandedness of Frow's eventual appeal to a dual perspective through the notion of the "ontological hybridity" of character, his understanding of the moral dimensions of literary representation remains underdeveloped and blunt, and when treating the experiential dimensions of reading and relating to characters, what he calls our "interest" in characters, he opts instead for a theory of identification based on a Freudian model and underwritten by the "narcissistic dissemination of ego-libido," which is claimed to be "the basis of all historically specific regimes of identification with fictional characters."[10] Emphasizing flexible identifications partly driven by psychological tendencies or needs seems to me worthwhile and important; reducing identification to psychological mechanisms of this sort demotes ethical practices and aims and subordinates their accompanying forms of self-cultivation to psychological drives, thereby participating in a broader subordination of moral commitment to psychological motives or constraints. I have discussed this feature of our field elsewhere, but it is important to note here since it forms part of the larger context in which the understanding of character at the present time must be situated.[11]

Interestingly, Frow at one point states that "a figural pattern asks us to respond to a form of life that we recognize," and it is in a formulation like this that I believe the more relevant issue appears.[12] Literary narratives engage us in forms of life, present us with ways of being, and they do so through complex formal means, one of which involves the presentation of ordinary thought processes, both momentary and sustained. It is precisely through the presentation of thinking and forms of consciousness that the phenomenology of reading coincides with, and is activated by, the form of thought represented. My premise is that these forms of thought, and in particular ruminative forms of thought, are not easy to convey in the novel or even, to some degree, in language.[13] Yet the novel has gone further than any other genre in developing ways to acknowledge and represent rumination. Free indirect discourse is one means of conveying it, as is stream of consciousness. But in the case of rumination what is difficult to convey is the circularity, the repetition, the resultlessness of thinking, where the repetition involved is not so much with a linguistic difference but with psychological differences, prompted by mood, by affective contingencies, by willfulness, by indifference and weakness of will, by distraction, and by the elusive workings of time itself, which can involve momentum, inertia, attrition, acceptance, or other effects.

Rumination as I define it, however, does involve some sort of orienting or nagging focus—a kind of obsession which for the present I want to defer judging as obsessive. Ruminations are also defined by what occasions them. They are the result of moral shock or disturbance: tragic occurrences, disgrace, status injury, injustice, alienation among friends or family members, and loss or threatened loss. They involve attempting to come to terms with these situations and often involve acute ethical dilemmas about how to act given competing claims or internal ambivalence. In this sense ruminations involve what I have elsewhere called moral time—the slow time of processing profound experiences.[14] My use of the term "moral time," like my use of the term "moral shock," is meant to underscore the close relation rumination bears to orienting values and commitments— the shock and the ruminative aftermath are often the result of a perceived violation of orienting values. A narrowly psychological understanding of rumination does not do justice to its fundamental moral dimension.

What is powerful about the novel's method of representing these forms of thought is its ability to capture their recurrence as well as the ways in which they can be nonteleological and yet somehow necessary to moments of punctual decision or processes of eventual acceptance or resignation. In this sense rumination must be contradistinguished from deliberation, that key processual form that has been used to attribute a living dynamic to the role of reason in politics and ethics. Rumination is not structured by sustained reflective awareness of the sort that we associate with deliberation. At the same time, however, it is characterized by persistence and repetition and a kind of attachment. It can be differentiated from the forms of thinking captured by the phrases "to ponder" or "to mull over," insofar as the first is typically used in relation to a highly focused and discrete problem or issue, and the second lacks the intensity and the attachment of rumination. "Preoccupation" might be the one word that comes closest to capturing its meaning. However, there are many ways beyond descriptive word choice in which writers and speakers convey the experience of rumination, as the examples I discuss will show.

The word "rumination" is not a prominent term in literary studies, in moral philosophy, or in the work in cognitive science and social psychology oriented toward questions of moral decision and moral justification. It is an established term in psychiatry and contemporary cognitive-behavioral psychology, however, where it signifies obsessive and circular thinking typically seen as pathological, and where it is also identified as a symptom of post-traumatic stress. Interestingly, *"ruminate"* stands out among the verbs that describe modes of thinking—verbs such as "contemplate," "reflect," "consider," "cogitate," "deliberate," "ponder," "muse," and "meditate"—in its etymological connection to nonhuman animals (the chewing of partially digested food among ruminants, such as the cow) and its use as a fundamentally pathological term in psychiatry. There is a further tendency, both within psychiatry and in common usage, to associate rumination with brooding, which in another meaning denotes the parental activity of instinctive care among bird species (incubating eggs by sitting atop them) but which when used figuratively is almost exclusively negative in connotation. These shades of meaning not only reveal biases but also stress the natural and everyday aspects of rumination as a part of ordinary moral and psychological life.

The complexity and potentiality of rumination as a form of moral thinking are seriously underrecognized. There is a longstanding tendency to read rumination psychologically and negatively (as fetish or symptom) rather than morally (as reparative or ameliorative). This situation is further enforced by the contemporary denigration of rumination in therapeutic culture, where it is seen as nonproductive and correctable through medication, though some recent psychological literature argues for differentiating between maladaptive and productive forms of rumination. The reconsideration of rumination within psychology appears to have been prompted by the acknowledgment of productive forms of focused, sustained thinking about one's troubles. In one study, for example, a distinction is drawn between brooding and reflection. Brooding is defined as "a passive comparison of one's current situation with some unachieved standard" and linked to the development of depression, anxiety disorders, post-traumatic stress, and eating disorders, among other psychopathologies. Reflection, by contrast, is "a purposeful turning inward to engage in cognitive problem solving to alleviate one's depressive symptoms."[15] In another study, four factors are specified—brooding, reflection, intrusive rumination, and deliberative rumination. Here reflection and deliberative rumination are considered adaptive, while brooding and intrusive rumination are considered maladaptive. Moreover, deliberative rumination is seen as a predictor of post-traumatic growth, a fascinating newer category in the psychological literature on trauma.[16]

A closer look at the distinctions drawn among the types of rumination in the four-factor analysis reveals some interesting assumptions, however. It turns out that attributions of negative and positive thought processes reify the definitions of intrusive and deliberative rumination. Brooding, linked primarily to depression, focuses on "symptoms of distress" in a presumptively reinforcing way. Intrusive rumination is oriented specifically toward negative aspects of a traumatic event, while deliberative rumination is associated with "attentional bias to positive information."[17] These distinctions raise several questions about what precisely rumination is imagined to be and in particular how one can distinguish it from other forms of thinking. Most problematically, intrusive rumination is imagined to be passive, while deliberative rumination is active and intentional. But this simple divide cannot capture the complexity of rumination, which often moves back and forth between negative and positive perspectives or attitudes. Ultimately, despite the apparent revisionism in psychology and the acknowledgment that rumination can promote post-traumatic growth, the newer analyses reinforce the pathological understanding of rumination, precisely by splitting off a positive conception of rumination and imposing cognitive-behavioral ideals on the field of ruminative thought. Rumination, even in its most productive forms, cannot be so easily captured or channeled.

If contemporary psychiatry and cognitive-behavioral psychology constitute a significant and somewhat distorting context for the contemporary understanding of rumination as a term and concept, contemporary cognitive science and social psychology have also significantly affected how we understand forms of thinking and their relation to moral action and moral decision. As I have discussed at greater length elsewhere, work in cognitive science and social psychology challenges longstanding conceptions of moral character and moral commitment.[18] Cognitive science research has served most notably and influentially as the basis for a dual-process theory of thinking, according to which the majority of our decisions take place not consciously but automatically, conditioned by forms of bias or by situational factors that "prime" our response. In Daniel Kahneman's *Thinking, Fast and Slow*, a framing distinction is made between the fast and more powerful System 1 (the automatic system) and the secondary System 2 (the slow, delibera-

tive system). Cognitive scientists have also advanced the claim
that moral judgments, often seen as inherently deliberative or
reflective, are actually automatic and intuitive, while carefully
constructed moral reasoning is post hoc. As Jonathan Haidt
argues in an influential survey of the experimental literature,
most moral reasoning takes place after the fact of intuitive judgment: "the reasoning process is more like a lawyer defending a
client than a judge or scientist seeking the truth."[19]

There are undeniably a myriad of ways in which we act un-
wittingly, automatically, and intuitively. The experiments de-
vised in the field of cognitive science, much like some of the
famous thought experiments in moral philosophy (e.g., the
trolley problem or the lifeboat dilemma), can disclose certain
dimensions of action and decision, but they are themselves con-
trived and highly susceptible to critique. To take one abiding
feature of these experiments, they typically involve responses
or actions taken in relation to strangers rather than familiars
of any sort. In this way alone they abstract from the embedded nature of our moral existence, which involves relations
within particular contexts and enduring over time. Being able
to demonstrate the existence of automatic decisions or intuitive judgments does not mean that what Kahneman calls "slow
thinking" is somehow merely secondary or less consequential
to our moral lives. The slow, reiterative quality of rumination,
its consideration and reconsideration of experiences of moral
shock and disturbance, of injury and loss, deeply informs the
ways in which individuals live their lives, confront their choices,
and define meaning and value for themselves and the commu-
nities to which they belong. And such values do not always express themselves in affirmative terms. The very "negativity" of
some ruminations is often the result of intensely felt injustice,
and their persistence is itself a form of commitment to social critique, as we shall see when we turn to the literary examples. In
their overattention to moments of decision in artificial settings,
the arguments about slow thinking or post hoc rationalizations

strangely miss the profound existential significance of rumination and in particular its consequential extension through time. Beyond this, the idea that the automatic processes are "fast" and deliberative processes are "slow" occludes the very important way in which certain slow, nondeliberative and semideliberative forms of thought are central to moral experience.[20]

Moral philosophy, too, emphasizes discrete moments of choice and decision as well as highly aware forms of deliberation and judgment, though it does so within a framework that privileges the processes that Kahneman relegates to the slow system. It is not wrong to pay attention to these dimensions of moral experience, for moral life significantly includes both decisive moments of deliberation and action and processes that take place silently and inwardly. As a focus on rumination shows, moments of moral decision, moral clarification, and moral epiphany take on their significance precisely within the context of profound processes that take place over time, including extended periods of anguished reflection, elusive processes of grief and healing, and gradual inner transformations as new perspectives emerge. Any reader of novels understands this, insofar as narratives are typically defined by dynamics between the punctual events and the longer processes that surround them. The very influential contemporary work in cognitive science, social psychology, and moral philosophy on forms of thinking, and in particular on their effect on our ongoing moral life, has thus far contributed very little to the understanding of rumination compared with the insights and capacities of novelistic form in this arena.

Despite this fact, the considerable role played by rumination in the novel has yet to receive due attention from literary studies itself. Interestingly, there is a certain affinity between cognitive science and prevailing assumptions within the literary field, despite the scientism of the former. Many influential claims in cognitive science reinforce from another direction the idea—familiar from poststructuralism, ideological criticism, and antihumanism—that we cannot lay claim to the forms of reflective human agency assumed in traditional moral frameworks. Within this context, there is little likelihood of rumination being recognized as at once psychologically and morally significant. In point of fact, most of the work exploring cognitive science in relation to literature has been trained on theory of mind and forms of cognition, and in particular on how they relate to reading practices and to the reading of other minds and human action within realist fiction. Moral questions have been to a large extent sidestepped in this literature, though they do appear in some scholarship on empathy and also in studies that explore storytelling and readerly experience within the framework of evolutionary psychology.[21] Vermeule's *Why Do We Care about Literary Characters?* falls into the latter category. It extends work done on the rise of the credit and contract economies in the eighteenth century, arguing that the novel during this important phase of historical development helped reading subjects hone their capacities to judge motive and position themselves advantageously within the new economy. For Vermeule, the novel as a genre permitted and promoted the development of Machiavellian intelligence in a new, atomized economic world. Yet to the extent that a study such as this addresses moral questions, it does so cynically. It is true that Vermeule focuses our attention on character as a crucial component of the novel's larger cultural project, and she also accords a certain empowered agency to the reader and to the writer. But what is lost to view is a broader conception of character that includes moral judgment and moral experience.[22]

In the remainder of this essay I explore the novel's interest in the complexity of moral thinking as it is lived in time, paying special attention to rumination as an understudied form of moral thinking characterized simultaneously by intermittence and persistence, distraction, and obsession. This means giving centrality to presentation of character, though it should be noted that forms of thinking in the novel are not exclusively the province of the character form. The narrative, and in some cases the narrator, can also figure importantly in the analysis. The English novel since its rise in the eighteenth century has explored dramas of the interior mental life (Defoe and Richardson present especially interesting examples), and certain nineteenth-century and twentieth-century writers have elaborated the moral psychology of rumination in distinctive ways, formally and conceptually.[23] I begin with a consideration of Eliot's references to rumination in *Middlemarch*, followed by a more extended reading of Trollope's *The Last Chronicle of Barset* and a somewhat briefer discussion of Woolf's *Mrs. Dalloway*. Trollope is arguably the one novelist in the realist British tradition who has most explored rumination in relation to moral life, and Woolf's novelistic art is uniquely trained on character and on the way thought travels, both within and beyond individual consciousness. Woolf is also fundamentally interested in experience within time, and I explore how *Mrs. Dalloway* engages the complex question of recurring thoughts and their relation to forms of duration as well as epiphanic modes of insight. By way of conclusion, I turn to Iris Murdoch's critique, in *The Sovereignty of Good*, of the overemphasis on choice and action in moral philosophy. Murdoch's recognition of the importance of time and duration to certain forms of moral reflection and insight is helpful in specifying the importance of rumination, even as her own concept of "attention" can and must be distinguished from it.

REALIST RUMINATIONS

An analysis of rumination in the novel does not depend upon direct uses of the term, though in certain cases such uses can be illuminating. Given the varying ways in which the term can and has been used, a narrowly lexical approach would be both constricting and misleading. In some cases, it is used as a near synonym for "reflect" or "meditate"; in others, aspects of abstraction or absorption are emphasized. And it is used by some novelists more than others. It appears hardly at all in Dickens's oeuvre, for example. The word appears once in *David Copperfield*, for instance, in the description of "the friendly waiter" David encounters when sent away from home: "he brought me a pudding, and having set it before me, seemed to ruminate, and to become absent in his mind for some moments. 'How's the pie?,' he said, rousing himself."[24] In Eliot's *Middlemarch*, it appears about a dozen times, usually with negative connotations, often gendered. A comparison of the word's appearances is in her case instructive, not only because it suggests that Eliot is attentive to varying resonances of the term but also because it illuminates larger concerns, both formal and thematic. When Madame Laure is surprised by Lydgate's following her to Paris, she is described as "looking at him with eyes that seemed to wonder as an untamed ruminating animal wonders."[25] And even more tellingly, the word is used in relation to Rosamond Vincy: "It had not occurred to Lydgate that he had been a subject of eager meditation to Rosamond, who had neither any reason for throwing her marriage into distant perspective, nor any pathological studies to divert her mind from that ruminating habit, that inward repetition of looks, words, and phrases, which makes a large part in the lives of most girls" (166). Fred Vincy's frustrated expectations generate "ruminations" as well, ones which produce "a streak of misanthropic bitterness" (119). And Casaubon ruminates unproductively on both his marriage and his health. But in Eliot not all ruminations are cast in these negative terms, as forms of thinking marked by deficiency, delusion, or resentment. There are two noteworthy instances where ruminations are viewed as productive of moral insight or resigned acceptance. One takes place during a discussion between Will and Dorothea, as Will is explaining Casaubon's dislike of him and also disclosing Casaubon's anxiety about others' judging him, which Will attributes to a self-doubt. Rather than jumping to Casaubon's defense, as she had in Rome, Dorothea remains quiet, and we are told that "the cause lay deep":

She was no longer struggling against the perception of facts, but adjusting them to her clearest perception; and now when she looked steadily at her husband's failure, still more at his possible consciousness of failure, she seemed to be looking along the one track where duty became tenderness. . . .

She did not answer at once, but after looking down ruminatingly she said, with some earnestness, "Mr. Casaubon must have overcome his dislike of you so far as his actions were concerned; and that is admirable." (365)

Here the brief ruminating activity seems to refer to the reinforcing perceptions accompanying her new sympathies for Casaubon, and it precedes a characteristic move toward placing Casaubon's actions toward Will in a positive light. In this case rumination is associated with an ongoing adjustment, one linked to moral growth in the face of difficult and hitherto unacknowledged aspects of her husband's character and abilities.

The second instance involves a comparison between Fred's and Farebrother's thought processes after the discussion in which Farebrother reassures Fred of his prospects for winning Mary Garth. Fred thanks Farebrother for what he has done, Farebrother responds graciously, and the narrator then describes the aftermath of the encounter:

In that way they parted. But both of them walked about a long while before they went out of the starlight. Much of Fred's rumination might be summed up in the words, "It certainly would have been a fine thing for her to marry Farebrother—but if she loves me best and I am a good husband?"

Perhaps Mr. Farebrother's might be concentrated into a single shrug and one little speech. "To think of the part one little woman can play in the life of a man, so that to renounce her may be a very good imitation of heroism, and to win her may be a discipline!" (676)

Foregrounded in this passage is the narrative choice to compress rumination into readable and clear statements, an understandable formal device given how long ruminative thought processes can extend (here, for "a long while") and how difficult they are to represent in clear communicative prose. It is interesting, in fact, that Eliot chooses balanced antitheses and the marking of both reductions as speech, typographically in both instances and explicitly in the second instance ("one little speech"). It is certainly the case that the formal representation of rumination, like the formal representation of stream of consciousness, presents challenges, both compositionally and aesthetically. Paul Ricoeur acknowledges this difficulty in *Time and Narrative*, signaling it as a major theoretical and formal question in a passage dealing with interior monologue: "To this 'magic' stemming from the direct reading of thoughts, this procedure adds the major difficulty of lending to a solitary subject the use of speech intended, in practical life, for communication—what in fact does talking to oneself mean? Leading the dialogic dimension of speech off its customary path for the benefit of soliloquy poses immense technical and theoretical problems that are not within my province here, but concern a study of the fate of subjectivity in literature."[26]

I shall return to this topic later in the discussions of Trollope and Woolf. For the present, however, it is worth noticing that Eliot here juxtaposes two types of rumination. Fred's belongs to the well-known psychological process of self-justification, and his summary statement can be inferred to duplicate the back-and-forth that marked his interior thought. The rumination can plausibly be seen, that is, as the unsettled, circular repetition in time of the very two-step movement captured in the statement. Farebrother's, by contrast, is not as easily recognizable as rumination at first glance, appearing more as a culminating ironic statement made in the wake of a deflating self-reflection. Not justification but rather its opposite: admission. But there is an important refection taking place, one which involves a psychological coming to terms with the gap between a decisive moral action and the psychological complexities and backlash that can accompany it. Indeed, Farebrother himself confesses to Fred that in speaking to him he is meaning to remain true to his own best intention, not allowing himself to be tempted by impulses to actively become Fred's rival. Rumination both precedes and follows this punctual moral act. It exists alongside the outward acts of moral life, and it can take moral commitment as the very object of its thinking. One might be tempted to say that what Eliot here calls rumination is simply deliberation, but the emphasis on the temporal extension and the psychological struggle argues for the distinctive form of ruminative thinking involved.

Also worthy of note here is the aphoristic form of this "little speech," one that is in keeping with the mode of the narrator, who often "concentrates" tensions between moral and psychological energies into knowing dicta of this sort, dicta which themselves contrast aspirational ideals with deflationary realities. Indeed, one could say that the narrative's own ruminative mode is of this very sort, endlessly moving back and forth between ennobling visions and sober realizations. Here then, moral epiphany is not an attempt to enforce moral certainty but rather a moment of insight situated in relation to ruminative processes that precede and follow it.

This discussion of the more positive references to rumination in Middlemarch reveals a form of moral thinking productive of profound forms of commitment and response, though rarely in a way that can be read in terms of sustained intention or understanding achieved through disciplined thinking. Although one can have disciplined habits of reflection that bespeak commitments (to better understanding, to one's own well-being, to loved ones who have died or suffered harm), much of what happens via rumination happens along the way, through unanticipated shifts of thinking, or realizations, or in a sudden opening of thought to a new perspective. Trollope, more than any other novelist in the nineteenth-century British tradition, acknowledges the centrality of ruminative thinking within moral and social life. He pays singular attention to forms of obsession in his characters, and he devotes considerable time to representing it. In the *Autobiography*, he famously asserts the importance of character over plot, and while he states that the focus on character allows for direct teaching of virtue and vice, he also voices the ambition to write characters realistically.[27] In a passage praising Hawthorne, he writes, "I have always desired 'to hew out some lump of the earth' and to make men and women walk upon it just as they do walk here among us."[28] And in fact his characters, even his "good" characters, are hardly simple paragons of virtue or honesty or courage. Indeed, his novels are noteworthy for the attention paid, often repeatedly in the case of a single character or situation, to subjective thought processes and interpersonal negotiations of unresolved dilemmas: the narrative consideration of such matters often seems to expand and dilate in an autotelic way, as though the pressure of plot progression has been utterly forgotten.

It is interesting that Trollope asserts in the *Autobiography* that in his view *The Last Chronicle of Barset* is the best novel he has written because it portrays "the mind of the unfortunate [Mr. Crawley] with great accuracy and delicacy."[29] Mr. Crawley is a victim of acute mind wandering, memory lapses, and various forms of what would today be viewed as cognitive impairment or decline. A poor and learned reverend who often struggles to feed his family, Mr. Crawley becomes suspected of the theft of a check he cashes. Apart from one notable exception, he repeatedly states that he cannot himself remember where he got it. The circle of people surrounding him, including all those closest to him, consider him innocent, though many believe he is innocent by virtue of insanity or compromised mental awareness. Vast portions of the narrative concern Crawley's mood and mental state, which are marked by fixation on the injustice of his poverty, the disrespect or "status injury" that poverty occasions, the waning powers of his mind, and the outrageous actions of Bishop Proudie and his domineering wife, Mrs. Proudie, who are attempting to prevent him from preaching at his church while his case is in limbo (having been advanced by the magistrates but not yet heard at the Assizes).

The representation of Mr. Crawley is a striking achievement in a body of work that is already notable for capturing obsessive postures and what I have elsewhere referred to as "recalcitrant psychologies."[30] It should be noted that Trollope's narrator both describes ruminative thought and attempts to show it through free indirect discourse. Thus, we might read a sentence such as "But the archdeacon went on thinking, thinking, thinking," or we may read an actual rumination of several pages.[31] Some of the characters also refer to their own ruminations and pass various forms of judgment on them. In what follows, I explore the way rumination of different kinds is distributed across the character-system (to borrow Woloch's useful concept) and what sort of interpretive claims an analysis of such thinking in Trollope might yield.

The Reverend Crawley displays persistent ruminative thinking, often described pejoratively by the narrator and other characters as "brooding." Indeed, his wife, who is presented as credibly aware of his ruminative obsessions, herself ruminates about his rumination. To give any flavor of Trollopian rumination, one must quote at some length. The following passage describes the aftermath of a scene in which Mrs. Crawley has sought to dissuade her husband from walking out to see his parishioners one morning, telling him she knows it will activate his brooding and leave him vulnerable to the cold, so insensible to his surroundings will he become. He sharply interrupts her, as it becomes clear that he realizes she fears he will commit suicide, either actively or passively; he assures her that she need fear nothing, and she relents:

> She did let him pass without another word, and he went out of the house, shutting the door after him noiselessly, and closing

the wicket-gate of the garden. For a while she sat herself down on the nearest chair, and tried to make up her mind how she might best treat him in his present state of mind. As regarded the present morning her heart was at ease. She knew that he would do now nothing of that which she had apprehended. She could trust him not to be false in his word to her, though she could not before have trusted him not to commit so much heavier a sin. If he would really employ himself from morning till night among the poor, he would be better so, —his trouble would be easier of endurance, —than with any other employment which he could adopt. What she most dreaded was that he should sit idle over the fire and do nothing. When he was so seated she could read his mind, as though it was open to her as a book. She had been quite right when she had accused him of over-indulgence in his grief. He did give way to it till it became a luxury to him, —a luxury which she would not have had the heart to deny him, had she not felt it to be of all luxuries the most pernicious. During these long hours, in which he would sit speechless, doing nothing, he was telling himself from minute to minute that of all God's creatures he was the most heavily afflicted, and was reveling in the sense of the injustice done to him. He was recalling all the facts of his life, his education, which had been costly, and, as regarded knowledge, successful; his vocation to the church, when in his youth he had determined to devote himself to the service of his Saviour, disregarding promotion or the favour of men; the short, sweet days of his early love, in which he had devoted himself again, —thinking nothing of self, but everything of her; his diligent working, in which he had ever done his very utmost for the parish in which he was placed, and always his best for the poorest; the success of other men who had been his compeers, and, as he too often told himself, intellectually his inferiors; then of his children, who had been carried off from his love to the churchyard, —over whose graves he himself had stood, reading out the pathetic words of the funeral service with unswerving voice and a bleeding heart; and then of his children still living, who loved their mother so much better than they loved him. And he would recall all the circumstances of his poverty,—how he had been driven to accept alms, to fly from creditors, to hide himself, to see his chairs and tables seized before the eyes of those over whom he had been set as their spiritual pastor. And in it all, I think, there was nothing so bitter to the man as the derogation from the spiritual grandeur of his position as priest among men, which came as one necessary result from his poverty. St. Paul could go forth without money in his purse or shoes to his feet or two suits to his back, and his poverty never stood in the way of his preaching, or hindered the veneration of the faithful. St. Paul, indeed, was called upon to bear stripes, was flung into prison, encountered terrible dangers. But Mr. Crawley,—so he told himself,—could have encountered all that without flinching. The stripes and scorn of the unfaithful would have been nothing to him, if only the faithful would have believed in him, poor as he was, as they would have believed in him had he been rich! Even they whom he had most loved treated him almost with derision, because he was now different from them. Dean Arabin had laughed at him because he had persisted in walking ten miles through the mud instead of being conveyed in the dean's carriage; and yet, after that, he had been driven to accept the dean's charity! No one respected him. No one! His very wife thought that he was a lunatic. And now he had been publicly branded as a thief; and in all likelihood would end his days in a gaol! Such were always his thoughts as he sat idle, silent, moody, over the fire; and his wife well knew their currents. It would certainly be better that he should drive himself to some employment, if any employment could be found possible to him.

When she had been alone for a few minutes, Mrs. Crawley got up from her chair, and going into the kitchen, lighted the fire there, and put the kettle over it, and began to prepare such breakfast for her husband as the means in the house afforded. (115–17)

This is a somewhat odd form of represented rumination, insofar as it is attributed, or second-order, rumination. But there are markers throughout that it is accurate attributed rumination, and at a certain point, by interjecting the phrase "I think," the narrator himself emphasizes what he takes to be the core insistent complaint, which creates an unusual effect of commentary on internal thought, a moment I will return to. In fact the passage moves among three perspectives in a seemingly untroubled way: the perspective of Mrs. Crawley, the narrator's perspective, and the interior thoughts of Mr. Crawley. For example, just as we are about to read the open book of Crawley's mind along with Mrs. Crawley, we read, "She had been quite right when she had accused him of over-indulgence in his grief." This sentence is written, it seems, from the narratorial perspective. But then we move, via free indirect discourse, back to Mrs. Crawley's thought stream: "He did give way to it [his grief], till it became a luxury to him, — a luxury which she would not have had the heart to deny him, had she not felt it to be of all luxuries the most pernicious." As we continue to read, sometimes Mr. Crawley's thoughts have an unmediated feel (as when he thinks of his children "who loved their mother so much better than they loved him"), and sometimes they are routed through the perspective of Mrs. Crawley or the narrator.

This passage of second-order rumination signals something important in this rather unsettling novel of a deteriorating, compromised, obsessive mind. First, the insertion of a credible intuitive and empathetic spouse lessens the extremity of Crawley's isolation, suggesting that his rumination is open to her, and serves as a powerful moral authority in his favor, both in the story world and for the reader. Otherwise, too much of that function would have to be carried by the narrator. And second, it belongs to a larger movement in the novel to domesticate, familiarize, and ultimately contain the rumination it nonetheless powerfully and rigorously represents. This movement is largely a response to the relentlessness of rumination and the psychological and social effects of that relentlessness.

The rumination itself discloses several key elements of Crawley's character relative to his circumstances. First of all, it is focused almost exclusively on status injury, the notion that he is not respected and recognized as he should be, given his position as a reverend, and given his learning and his devotion to both his calling and his family. He is also wounded by awareness that his children prefer their mother and by his wife's perception of his madness. In general, given that we receive this rumination by means of Mrs. Crawley's second-order rumination, we are asked to judge Mr. Crawley's thought processes as indulgent and nonproductive—"maladaptive" in the language of contemporary psychology. And yet, it is interestingly the case that this moody obsession with status also reveals something important about the indignities of a social world that despises poverty, and therefore, it indirectly advances a critique of the forms of hypocrisy in a putatively religious society. The fact that the narrator intervenes at just the moment that this obsessive focus is elaborated makes this aspect of the passage more pronounced. Indeed, the narrator makes a point of identifying poverty as the cause of Crawley's injured status: "And in it all, I think, there was nothing so bitter to the man as the derogation from the spiritual grandeur of his position as priest among men, which came as one necessary result from his poverty." The bitterness of Crawley's response to his situation, which might draw a moral judgment from Mrs. Crawley or from the narrator, is nonetheless and importantly the result of an objective sociological fact: poverty invites and allows disrespect. Through its shifting and complex presentation, then, the novel asks us to do several things at once: evaluate the rumination as nonproductive; recognize the suffering of Mr. Crawley; and perceive how social violence instigates ruminative processes as the individual aims to come to terms with ongoing harm.

Another layer of meanings is added by the focalization through Mrs. Crawley, who combines sympathy, concern, and judgment in her meditation on her husband's state of mind. Strikingly, we are told that when he is seated by the fire, "she could read his mind, as though it was open to her as a book."

Such a moment seems to suggest that Mrs. Crawley is a reader-surrogate, bringing a sympathetic, discerning judgment to bear upon the complexities of a suffering mind. It also elevates the novel form as a window into ruminative processes, an effect underscored when the narrator intrudes. Both Mrs. Crawley and the narrator treat Mr. Crawley's thinking with respect, replicating and explaining it. And the reference made to everyday life as Mrs. Crawley proceeds to her daily tasks reveals that the form of devotion she shows in thinking about her husband's thinking is one that will repeat itself daily. There is thus within this very passage an acknowledgment of two different forms of rumination, but they do not follow the pattern suggested in the psychological literature. If it is true that we can call Mr. Crawley's ruminations negative, something to be avoided through activity and exertion, it is not the case that we can simply call Mrs. Crawley's thinking "positive." It is rather at once realistic (authorized by the narrative as accurate) and devotional, a form of commitment that will repeat itself, one that carries value but will in no way resolve anything.

After Mr. Crawley, the character who arguably is most caught up in a ruminative process is Lily Dale, who is repeatedly asked to consider whether she will marry Johnny Eames, a longtime suitor. Lily is in love with another man, Adolphus Crosbie, whose jilting of her is recounted in the novel directly preceding *The Last Chronicle of Barset*, *The Small House at Allington*. In the *Last Chronicle*, Lily learns that the heiress for whom Crosbie abandoned her has died and that Crosbie is free again. He attempts to test the waters by writing to Lily's mother. At the same time, Johnny continues to press his suit, with the support of many in Lily's circle. Lily refers to her ruminations on the matter repeatedly (though the word is not used). Of course, this interestingly lights up the fact that deliberations about possible suitors is a key feature of the realist novel, particularly in the eighteenth and nineteenth centuries, just as marriage, or deliberation brought to a close, is a common vehicle of plot closure.

Other characters who notably ruminate include Archdeacon Grantly, an authoritarian father prone to fits of anger; his son, Henry Grantly, who has fallen in love with Mr. Crawley's daughter Grace and agonizes over whether it is right or not to defy his father and marry her, an act which could bring disgrace upon his family by association; and Grace Crawley herself, who agonizes over how to respond to Henry Grantly in both imagined and real exchanges. All these ruminations, like the ruminations of Mr. and Mrs. Crawley, are occasioned by an experience of moral shock or disturbance: in the case of Lily Dale, betrayal and heartbreak; in the case of Archdeacon Grantly, offended honor and filial disobedience; in the case of Henry Grantly, threatened loss and familial alienation; and in the case of Grace Crawley, a disturbed desire not to bring dishonor upon Henry Grantly. Trollope consistently registers the ways in which rumination can be unproductive, but he also acknowledges its force, its unavoidability. Beyond this, he juxtaposes a form of devotional rumination to these unproductive tendencies, as we saw already in the case of Mrs. Crawley. The manner in which Trollope approaches the difficulties attaching to rumination (its solipsism, its negative dimensions, and its more redemptive forms) can best be seen through the divergent ways in which ruminative behavior plays out with respect to Mr. Crawley, on the one hand, and Lily Dale, on the other. If the literature on cognitive science distorts moral life through the conclusions it draws from punctual experiments that fail to capture experience in time, the novel has its own formal constraints as well, and individual novelists have their own value systems—these factors can combine to situate rumination in ways that also might be said to variously limit or light up its lived ongoingness.

As it happens, Mr. Crawley is rescued from his suffering through a plot disclosure. It turns out that when Crawley's friends, the Arabins, had helped him with money, Mrs. Arabin had secretly augmented the gift with a check that had been given to her but that she didn't know had been stolen. Dean Arabin therefore never knew the check had been passed on to Mr. Crawley by his wife. And while Mr. Crawley's memory was genuinely unsteady, he is also said to have been unable to contradict Dean Arabin's claim that he did not give Crawley the check: we are told Crawley could not trust his recollection (in moments of clarity) that the dean had in fact given him the check because he could not believe the dean capable of any form of error or dishonesty. (This situation is also the result of a cultural tendency to simply consider the wife's action an extension of the husband's, when in this case the wife acted independently.) With the disclosure by Mrs. Arabin of the truth, moral integrity as a form of anchored character underwrites the end of the novel, vindicating Crawley and Crawley's conception of the dean. The threat of cognitive decline, mind wandering, and what is sometimes in the novel referred to as partial madness thus recedes and allows for an assured moral agency enduring in character. In addition, Crawley is rescued from his brooding-inducing poverty through the gift of a more handsome living, and we are told that "soon after that, Mr. and Mrs. Crawley became quiet at St. Ewold's, and, as I think, contented" (857). The ruminative hum has subsided. Alternatively, one might see this as a transfer of ruminative roles, where the narratorial task—marked by "as I think"—replaces the characterological burden.

In the case of Lily, she at once acknowledges and forswears rumination, noting how miserable it has made her. Earlier she had rebuked her mother for stating that her history with Adolphus Crosbie was best not discussed, since "the memory of [certain things] should not be fostered by much talking." Lily replies:

> To talk of forgetting such an accident as that is a farce. And as for fostering the memory of it—! Do you think that I have ever spent a night from that time to this without thinking of him? Do you imagine that I have ever crossed our own lawn, or gone down through the garden-path there, without thinking of the times

when he and I walked there together? There needs no fostering for such memories as these. There are weeds which will grow rank and strong though nothing be done to foster them. There is the earth and the rain, and that is enough for them. You cannot kill them if you would, and they certainly will not die because you are careful not to hoe and rake the ground. (229)

Lily here insists upon the naturalness as well as the force of rumination upon powerful loss (in calling the thoughts "weeds," she casts them as both natural and destructive). By the end of the novel, Lily has become almost bitter about the effects of rumination, which in her rebuke to her mother she owns as unavoidable but also describes as frustratingly beyond her control, something she cannot help. For example, when encouraged by a friend to reconsider Johnny Eames, to "think of it," Lily responds, "I have thought of it. I have thought of nothing else. I am tired of thinking of it. It is not good to think of anything so much. What does it matter?" (790).

Still, "thinking of it," and doing so over time, has led her to the commitment not to marry. And, interestingly, Lily's way of describing her ruminations about whether or not to marry Johnny—a question intimately bound up with thinking about Adolphus Crosbie too—is very different from her way of describing the lingering heartbreak surrounding Crosbie, the weeds she cannot avoid and that will intrude no matter what. In talking with Emily Dunstable of her ruminations about Johnny, she associates them with a "state of doubt" that has left her unable to do anything and that has lasted "six or eight months." They are prompted—or triggered, to use a more contemporary idiom—anytime someone starts talking about Johnny. But she goes on to say, "And yet all along I have known how it would be—as well as I do now" (798).

In both her final conversation with Johnny and her conversation with Emily Dunstable, we get a sense of what the time of doubt mixed with certainty represents, both for Lily and within the novel's own presentation of thinking in the context of defining moral experiences. With an honesty and directness unmatched in any other conversations on the matter, even those with her mother, Lily tells Johnny that even though she no longer loves Crosbie, she cannot marry Johnny: "If you take a young tree and split it, it still lives perhaps. But it isn't a tree. It is only a fragment" (797). Lily has been changed unalterably by the experience of Crosbie's desertion, and she will never marry. But something else is also disclosed as she speaks of Johnny to Emily: she loves him with an "intimate, close, familiar affection" (798), but cannot be his wife. She goes on to say she could wash his clothes for him, as earlier she had said she would tend him when sick. There is a kind of sororal devotion here born of a long history, a history defined by loyalty and commitment and ongoing everydayness. This suggests that Lily's extended "state of doubt" is a crucial form of commitment, both to her own values and to Johnny, one that can be expressed only over time. We all know that there are some requests so weighty that one must honor them by taking time to think about them, even if one knows all along "how it would be." But this is something more than such a form of respect: it is a partly intentional, partly endured ruminative span that constitutes a form of devotion not unlike the simple everyday acts one does for others, such as washing their clothes or, as in Mrs. Crawley's case, making breakfast.

After Lily's decision is finalized and communicated, the narrator intervenes to create an unusual effect of liveness:

> On the next day Lily Dale went down to the Small House of Allington, and so she passes out of our sight. I can only ask the reader to believe that she was in earnest, and express my own opinion, in this last word that I shall ever write respecting her, that she will live and die as Lily Dale. (798)[32]

Here, Trollope reinforces the artificiality of closure in the case of a novelistic rendering of a life committed to thoughtful awareness and lived commitment. But precisely in refusing the conventional end of a romance plot, he also asks us to consider a form of ongoing ordinary life that is rich in ruminative thought, even as both he and the character conspire in producing an enforced stop to this train of thought that ends only with death. Thus, Trollope manages to evoke a ruminative afterlife for his plot and so to honor what Hannah Arendt, in "Thinking and Moral Considerations," refers to as a necessarily "resultless" enterprise. As she puts it, "The need to think can be satisfied only through thinking, and the thoughts which I had yesterday will be satisfying this need today only to the extent that I can think them anew."[33]

EPIPHANY AND RUMINATION IN MODERNISM

Modernism is associated with striking formal innovations in the representation of interior thought, and one might expect that it would therefore be a rich site of inquiry for the study of rumination, perhaps richer than the realist novel. It is important, however, to distinguish between stream of consciousness as a whole and rumination. Stream of consciousness, in its aim to capture the often nonlinear, idiosyncratic, and overdetermined aspects of everyday consciousness, certainly captures many of the characteristic features associated with rumination. But rumination has distinct elements as a form of moral reflection and, most crucially, is occasioned by an attempt to come to terms with an instigating moral shock. Insofar as it does so, moreover, it is critically oriented toward interpersonal and social contexts, however solipsistic it may seem. For this reason, rumination troubles any notion that the modernist move inward involves a move away from the social.[34] And it allows us to make distinctions among different modernist novels. The obsessive and circular thought patterns of Beckett's narrators capture formal elements that are also at play in rumination (repetition, distraction, nagging focus), but in their cognitive solipsism they often do not prominently involve the distinctive moral conditions and features of rumination.[35] Virginia Woolf's novels, by contrast, centrally display morally and socially consequential forms of rumination. In this section of the essay, I will argue for the importance of rumination in *Mrs. Dalloway* and then by way of conclusion turn to the philosophical work of Iris Murdoch in order to further elucidate Woolf's novelistic vision as well as the larger stakes of the study of rumination.

Mrs. Dalloway takes the relations among interior thought, death, and time as its subject. What is striking in the novel is the contrast between punctual, epiphanic moments of affirmation and time-laden processes such as everyday ritual, distracted or rote behaviors, and ruminative thought. Two traumatic events—two experiences of moral shock—structure the most prominent recursive thought processes within the novel. For Septimus Warren, who will commit suicide in the course of the day whose events the novel records, the experience of the Great War, including the death of a fellow soldier and friend, alters his view of life, and his relations with others, irrevocably and negatively. For Clarissa Dalloway and Peter Walsh, the painfully determining event in both their lives is the end of their youthful romantic relationship, which results when Clarissa decides to marry Richard Dalloway, a conventional public servant, instead of the intellectual and energetically critical Peter Walsh, with whom she has an uncanny bond. On the day of the novel's events, Peter is visiting London from India, where he lives and works. He remains haunted by Clarissa, both by his prior love for her and by the experience of the break, which, in his words, "had spoilt his life."[36] It is not unlike the situation of Lily Dale even though he now, after many years, has concrete plans to marry. Still, for him the fact remains: "One could not be in love twice" (192). Clarissa herself is not free of pain over her own choice. Even though "she was convinced" the break was necessary, "she had borne about with her for years like an arrow sticking in her heart the grief, the anguish" (9).

The lasting effects of the break between Peter and Clarissa contrast with the novel's emphasis on epiphanies of felt connection and heightened appreciation of everyday life. Clarissa feels a sense of indebtedness to "this secret deposit of exquisite moments" (29), acknowledging that one must make an effort to repay them. Her party is in some sense a form of homage to this very conception of life, one that values eventfulness and human connection, whether new and unexpected or in relation to contexts of longer duration. Ruminative experiences oriented toward loss and regret are the painful background, to some extent, of these moments of grace.[37]

The quality and object of Clarissa's and Peter's ruminations are different, as are their moments of inspiration and consolation. To some extent, Clarissa is subject to the very form of rumination defined by contemporary psychiatry. She has a sense that her motivation for action is simply to impress others, and yet she also feels that "no one was ever for a second taken in." She compares herself negatively with Richard, who "did things for themselves" (10). Beyond this, she finds herself caught up in feelings of intense dislike for Miss Kilman, her daughter's friend and spiritual mentor, who is at once a "poor embittered unfortunate creature" and "one of those spectres with which one battles in the night" (12). Clarissa moves back and forth between experiencing disgust for Miss Kilman and berating herself for experiencing that disgust, in a classic two-step movement of ruminative thinking. Miss Kilman also ruminates, resenting the fact that Clarissa would never think to ask her to her party, resenting also how Clarissa makes her feel:

> It was the flesh that she must control. Clarissa Dalloway had insulted her. That she expected. But she had not triumphed; she had not mastered the flesh. Ugly, clumsy, Clarissa Dalloway had laughed at her for being that; and had revived fleshly desires, for she minded looking as she did beside Clarissa. Nor could she talk as she did. But why wish to resemble her? Why? She despised

Mrs. Dalloway from the bottom of her heart. She was not serious. She was not good. Her life was a tissue of vanity and deceit. Yet Doris Kilman had been overcome. She had, as a matter of fact, very nearly burst into tears when Clarissa Dalloway laughed at her. "It is the flesh, it is the flesh," she muttered (it being her habit to talk aloud) trying to subdue this turbulent and painful feeling as she walked down Victoria Street. She prayed to God. She could not help being ugly; she could not afford to buy pretty clothes. Clarissa had laughed—but she would concentrate her mind upon something else until she had reached the pillar-box. At any rate she had got Elizabeth. But she would think of something else; she would think of Russia; until she reached the pillar-box. (129)

Woolf's free indirect discourse conveys a bluntness to Miss Kilman's thoughts, which are rendered in staccato prose and which, unlike the thought processes of Clarissa, are vulgarized through direct speech ("it being her habit to talk aloud") and through convention in the form of religious doctrine. Miss Kilman recurs over and over again to the feeling of injured status and tries repeatedly to redirect her thoughts, to avoid sinful impulses. Indeed, this whole passage conveys how routinized certain forms of rumination are within religious practices of confession, repentance, and self-castigation. Clarissa's own thought processes share some of the features of Miss Kilman's, but they are rendered in elegant, rhythmic phrases:

How many million times she had seen her face, and always with the same imperceptible contraction! She pursed her lips when she looked in the glass. It was to give her face point. That was her self—pointed; dartlike; definite. That was her self when some effort, some call on her to be her self, drew the parts together, she alone knew how different, how incompatible and composed so for the world only into one centre, one diamond, one woman who sat in her drawing-room and made a meeting-point, a radiancy no doubt in some dull lives, a refuge for the lonely to come to, perhaps; she had helped young people, who were grateful to her, had tried to be the same always, never showing a sign of all the other sides of her—faults, jealousies, vanities, suspicions, like this of Lady Bruton not asking her to lunch; which she thought (combing her hair finally), is utterly base! Now where was her dress? (37)

Clarissa's mind evinces a less bluntly self-chastising form of self-awareness and is accorded a more elevated prose, but nonetheless one can discern the same ruminative patterns— self-assessment, self-critique, registration of status injury, and self-protective response (via either self-justification or self-protecting distraction).

What rescues the process of negative rumination, and does so unevenly across the character-system, is the epiphanic moment. Typically, the insight seems a mere gift of the moment—a spiritual experience or a form of belonging acutely felt. Clarissa is the privileged figure here, with her culminating feeling of connection at day's end with the old woman across the way, seen from her window. Her thoughts about the reason she loves to give parties also privilege the forms of resonance that unscripted moments of connection yield. Peter Walsh, by contrast, displays a tendency to evade and denigrate rumination even as he cannot escape the thought of Clarissa: "she kept coming back and back like a sleeper jolting against him in a railway carriage" (76). And his moments of affirmation are keyed not to an appreciation of the everyday, as in Clarissa's case, but to an ego-fortifying sense of the value of England and of civilization. In this sense the rhythm of his thinking has some affinities with the forms of complacency represented by Sir William Bradshaw, who asserts the value of "proportion" against what he sees as the indulgences or weaknesses of others.[38] And yet Peter is also highly critical of Clarissa's conventionality and worldliness, and her awareness of this critique acts as a kind of pressure on her own ruminations. The problem is that Peter does not want to examine himself. His ruminations are about trying to explain Clarissa—how she could have chosen Richard Dalloway, how she can be the extraordinary force she remains while having settled into a conventional existence, one that privileges "rank and society and getting on in this world" (76). And they are also about acknowledging the effects of time on his ways of thinking and his relations with others—in particular, time's attenuating effect on his interest in, and sense of connection to, others. But when his thoughts turn more directly inward, he often evades and disavows the ruminative mode:

> There was Regent's Park. Yes. As a child he had walked in Regent's Park—odd, he thought, how the thought of childhood keeps coming back to me—the result of seeing Clarissa, perhaps; for women live much more in the past than we do, he thought. They attach themselves to places; and their fathers—a woman's always proud of her father. (55)

In a sense, Peter's moments of intensified feeling are all mediated through Clarissa, and his keen sense of loss involves not only the loss of her but also the loss of an immediacy of connection, one that is figured in their ability, still active after so many years of separation, to conduct what can only be called internal dialogues. These are some of the strangest moments in the text, and they share some of the quality of Mrs. Crawley's second-order rumination. Peter meditates at one point on the fact that "they always had this queer power of communicating without words" (60), musing on the fact that her sense that he is internally criticizing her often instigates their vocal quarrels. Woolf represents several of these silent dialogues in the narrative as well. This feature of the text underscores the profoundly social context of interior thought in Woolf, one that encompasses both intimacy and antagonism.

Despite its rich consideration of rumination's moral and social contexts, however, *Mrs. Dalloway* ultimately presents a suspended dialectic between epiphany and rumination: epiphany saves one from the solipsism, antagonism, and resultlessness of everyday thought as it circles around regret, loss, and injured vanity. Rumination here is negatively presented. This can be contrasted with the forms of moral change half-earned and half-effected over time through the long slow processes of ruminative commitment, as we saw with Lily Dale in *The Last Chronicle of Barset*.[39] But in Trollope, of course, the example of Lily Dale is offset by the critique of Mr. Crawley's unproductive brooding. An implicit or explicit devaluation of negative rumination is a common feature in writers who significantly represent the terrain of rumination, and any comprehensive treatment of the topic will require an engagement with the ongoing tendency to produce an evaluative distinction between the two. The preliminary question to ask in any given case is whether the distinction helps us to see the full complexity of the ruminative process and how capaciously it can embrace the importance of the full range of ruminative modes and, especially, their relation to time-laden moral transformations.

RUMINATION AND ATTENTION: CONCLUDING THOUGHTS

Iris Murdoch's work on forms of attention can usefully illuminate the issues raised by the enduring tendency to divide rumination into good and bad forms. Murdoch is an important figure for the study of rumination because her own work on moral reflection starts from the premise, shared by this essay, that an overattention to decision and choice will limit our understanding of moral experience, some of which takes place through slow processes whose duration is significant for their effect.[40] Murdoch develops a concept of attention that is meant to characterize moments of sudden insight as well as forms of sustained reflection that are morally meaningful in their capacity to shift one's understanding of another person or situation. While too ongoingly deliberative to capture the full dimensions of rumination as I define it, Murdoch's conception of attention importantly discloses the significance of forms of interior mental experience that do not eventuate in any discernible public action or announced decision.

Strikingly, one can discern a certain version of unproductive rumination, deliberately contrasted with attention, at play in Murdoch's overall schema. This can be seen most clearly if one contrasts the first essay in *The Sovereignty of Good*, "The Idea of Perfection," with the final essay, "The Sovereignty of Good." The latter essay aims to draw out how different modes of attention can be said to be virtuous, or oriented toward the good. From appreciation of nature, to intellectual work, to experiences of art, we encounter modes of attention that help us to move away from ongoing human tendencies of selfish and anxious preoccupation toward forms of virtue. For Murdoch, these ennobling forms of attention and cultivated practice are defined against a steady default state in which consciousness is a "cloud of more or less fantastic reverie designed to protect the psyche from pain."[41] In the first example in the essay, when distraction from self is prompted by an experience of singular natural beauty, the ordinary stream of thought preceding the event condenses the several negative forms of rumination with which we are by now familiar: "I am looking out of my window in an anxious and resentful state of mind, oblivious of my surroundings, brooding perhaps on some damage done to my prestige. Then suddenly I observe a hovering kestrel. In a moment everything is altered. The brooding self with its hurt vanity has disappeared. There is nothing now but kestrel. And when I return to the other matter it seems less important" (82).

If here Murdoch contrasts a moment of surprised attention with negative, self-involved consciousness, "The Idea of Perfection" elaborates and defends forms of moral attention that the tradition of moral philosophy, focused as it is on discrete judgments and forms of publicly visible action, has failed to recognize, or has recognized only to denigrate. Through the concept of attention, Murdoch describes and honors inward moral activity sustained over time. The central example involves a mother-in-law's changing attitude toward her daughter-in-law. Murdoch designates the two figures M and D, respectively. M engages in an active attempt to rethink or reframe her perceptions of D, whom she had earlier seen as vulgar and somewhat juvenile. Over the course of a few years she comes to see her differently (the daughter-in-law is, for the sake of the example, assumed absent or dead). She becomes instead someone with a spirited energy, "delightfully youthful" (17). The activity of M's rethinking her understanding of D is taken by Murdoch to be important and serious moral work, and yet it cannot be recognized by traditional moral philosophy of the "behaviorist, existentialist, and utilitarian" sort (8), nor can it be seen within a Kantian framework. Actively motivated by the desire to see justly and lovingly, it involves ongoing, private practices of reflection that share a resemblance to the morally consequential forms of rumination I have been describing in this essay.

Herself both a philosopher and a novelist, Murdoch builds her case for the significance of moral attention by reference to the genre of the novel. When discussing M's effort to reimagine D, she writes, "Innumerable novels contain accounts of what such struggles are like" (22). This is certainly the case, but it is also the case that innumerable novels capture the less deliberative processes of rumination as well. It is important to underscore here that rumination is not ongoingly "attentive" in the way that Murdoch imagines it. It has a nagging focus and ebbs and flows in intensity and degree of awareness, but its intermittence is also important to the time-laden essence of its processual nature, which can be described as neither passive nor active, neither intrusive nor deliberate, but instead remains a curious mixture of the two. And crucially, there are often ways in which what we think of as unproductive rumination and productive rumination are bound up in one another. Murdoch's identification of default habits of thought that are brooding, solipsistic, and vain plays into the tendency to identify and devalue a clearly negative form of rumination. Similarly, her contrast of moments of epiphany with an ongoing undertow of self-involved thinking is not unlike the arrested dialectic at play in Woolf. But Murdoch's treatment of hard-won moral shifts, as well as ongoing attempts to cultivate an open, just, and loving mind, cannot be described this way. And her treatment of the importance of the slow time of certain moral experiences is directly relevant to the theorization of rumination.

That theorization, as this essay has aimed to show, can be advanced through an attentive reading of the novelistic tradition and relies centrally on readings of character. I use the word "attentive" advisedly. Murdoch's concept of attention is applicable not only to certain strenuous moral efforts but also to the focused activities of readers and critics who are actively reading portrayals of rumination and other forms of moral reflection.[42] Readers may be invited to attend to patterns of rumination in the novel or emanating from the narrative itself. Narrators can themselves have a ruminative relation to certain themes, as we saw in the case of Eliot's narrator, whose philosophical musings repeatedly circle around idealism and its deflation. Beyond this, readers may be drawn into ruminative thought streams precisely via their own sense of identification with them. In this sense, a better understanding of rumination may allow for a deepened phenomenology of reading, a task crucial in a cultural context in which cognitive science frameworks are playing a dominant and distorting role.

Given the novel's interest in broad social contexts and themes, moreover, a literary-critical exploration of rumination can show us the crucial social and political dimensions of ruminative processes, especially those that tend to be denigrated in moral and psychological terms. As the example of Mr. Crawley shows, Trollope invites us to attend to the social context of his status injury, what today we would call its structural dimensions. Brooding, injured characters within the novel often perform this function. Sometimes the writers participate in pathologizing them and sometimes they don't, but the ongoing injury of social disenfranchisement is often powerfully represented through characterological rumination, and a study of this aspect of the novelistic corpus is utterly vital to a fuller understanding of the novel as a moral and sociopolitical form.

An acknowledgment and analysis of rumination will allow us to better account for both the moral dimension of fiction and the forms of thinking that characterize moral and political life more broadly. Such an analysis is premised on the notion that attention to character and the character-system is crucial to this task. Approaching this dimension of the novel requires that we work in and through character, as both a literary and a moral concept. To return to the point at which I started, and to underscore one of Woolf's central points in "Mr. Bennett and Mrs. Brown," this kind of criticism requires a more forthright and noncynical acknowledgment of our profound interest in character as we read.

NOTES

The development of this essay was helped immeasurably by conversations with audiences at the Duke University PAL workshop in March 2018, the SCT Conference at New York University in April 2018, and the Society for Novel Studies conference at Cornell University in June 2018. I am especially indebted to conversations with Branka Arsić and careful readings of earlier drafts by Rita Felski and Toril Moi. I also want to add a special thanks to Gregory Chase, who served as respondent at the PAL workshop, and to Toril Moi, for suggesting the relevance of Murdoch's concept of attention to the topic of rumination.

1. Virginia Woolf, "Mr. Bennett and Mrs. Brown," in *The Hogarth Essays* (New York: Doubleday, 1928), 5.

2. Ibid., 6.

3. Ibid., 12–13.

4. Ibid., 4–5.

5. I borrow the phrase "counted on" from Paul Ricoeur, who uses it to great effect when describing ethics in life and literature. See Paul Ricoeur, *Oneself as Another*, trans. Kathleen Blamey (Chicago: University of Chicago Press, 1992), 165.

6. Woolf, "Mr. Bennett and Mrs. Brown," 9.

7. Alex Woloch, *The One vs. the Many: Minor Characters and the Space of the Protagonist in the Novel* (Princeton, NJ: Princeton University Press, 2003); John Frow, *Character and Person* (Oxford: Oxford University Press, 2014); Blakey Vermeule, *Why Do We Care about Literary Characters?* (Baltimore: Johns Hopkins University Press, 2010).

8. Paul Ricoeur argues in *Time and Narrative* for the centrality of character, and of the thoughts and feelings of the character, to the novel: "The narrated world is the world of the characters and it is narrated by the narrator. The notion of character is solidly anchored in narrative theory to the extent that a narrative cannot be a mimesis of action without being at the same time a mimesis of acting beings. And acting beings are, in the broad sense that the semantics of action confers on the notion of an agent, beings who think and feel—better, beings capable of talking about their thoughts, their feelings, and their actions. It is thus possible to shift the notion of mimesis from the action toward the character, and from the character toward the character's discourse. . . . The question will then be to determine by which special narrative means the narrative is constituted as *the discourse of a narrator recounting the discourse of the characters*. The notions of point of view and of narrative voice designate two of these means." Paul Ricoeur, *Time and Narrative*, vol. 2, trans. Kathleen McLaughlin and David Pellauer (Chicago: University of Chicago Press, 1985), 88 (emphasis in the original).

9. Frow, *Character and Person*, 16–17.

10. Ibid., 52.

11. Amanda Anderson, *Psyche and Ethos: Moral Life after Psychology*, Clarendon Lectures in English (Oxford: Oxford University Press, 2018).

12. Frow, *Character and Person*, 36.

13. The question of whether certain forms of thought take place outside language is a complex one, with a history of arguments for and against. For an overview of the arguments that language is not necessary for thought, see Iain McGilchrist, *The Master and His Emissary: The Divided Brain and the Making of the Western World* (New Haven, CT: Yale University Press, 2009), 106–10.

14. See Anderson, *Psyche and Ethos*.

15. Wendy Treynor, Richard Gonzalez, and Susan Nolen-Hoeksema, "Rumination Reconsidered: A Psychometric Analysis," *Cognitive Therapy and Research* 27, no. 3 (2003): 256.

16. Felipe E. García, Felix Cova, and Almudena Duque, "The Four Faces of Rumination to Stressful Events: A Psychometric Analysis," *Psychological Trauma: Theory, Research, Practice, and Policy* 9, no. 6 (2017): 758.

17. Ibid., 759.

18. Anderson, *Psyche and Ethos*.

19. See Daniel Kahneman, *Thinking, Fast and Slow* (New York: Farrar, Straus and Giroux, 2011); Jonathan Haidt, "The Emotional Dog and Its Rational Tail: A Social Intuitionist Approach to Moral Judgment," *Psychological Review* 108, no. 4 (2001): 820. Also see Anderson, *Psyche and Ethos*, 21–23.

20. See Anderson, *Psyche and Ethos*, 39–53.

21. For a discussion of empathy, see Paul Armstrong, *How Literature Plays with the Brain: The Neuroscience of Reading and Art* (Baltimore: Johns Hopkins University Press, 2013), 158–62.

22. See Anderson, *Psyche and Ethos*, 36–37.

23. Rumination as a feature of the novel is of course not limited to the English tradition, and this analysis could profitably be extended beyond the preliminary examples I present here. One primary example from twentieth-century American literature is Toni Morrison's *Beloved*, but there are many more, a number of which I am exploring in a larger project on this topic.

24. Charles Dickens, *David Copperfield* (New York: Penguin, 1996), 71.

25. George Eliot, *Middlemarch* (New York: Penguin, 1994), 152. Hereafter page numbers will be given parenthetically in the text.

26. Ricoeur, *Time and Narrative*, 2:90 (see also n. 13 above).

27. This paragraph is drawn from the opening of Amanda Anderson, "Trollope's Modernity," *ELH* 74 (2007): 509–10.

28. Anthony Trollope, *An Autobiography* (Oxford: Oxford University Press, 1998), 145.

29. Ibid., 274.

30. Anderson, "Trollope's Modernity."

31. Anthony Trollope, *The Last Chronicle of Barset* (New York: Penguin, 2002), 350. Hereafter page numbers will be given parenthetically in the text.

32. Interestingly, in the *Autobiography* (178–79), Trollope makes the following remarks about Lily Dale, at first strongly distancing himself from her, but then seeming to acknowledge the powerful force of her ruminative commitment to her first love: "In the love with which she has been greeted I have hardly joined with much enthusiasm, feeling that she is somewhat of a French prig. She became first engaged to a snob, who jilted her; and then, though in truth she loved another man who was hardly good enough, she could not extricate herself sufficiently from the collapse of her first great misfortune to be able to make up her mind to be the wife of one whom, though she loved him, she did not altogether reverence. Prig as she was, she made her way into the hearts of many readers, both young and old; so that, from that time to this, I have been continually honored with letters, the purport of which has always been to beg me to marry Lily Dale to Johnny Eames. Had I done so, however, Lily would never have so endeared herself to these people as to induce them to write letters to the author concerning her fate. It was because she could not get over her troubles that they loved her."

33. Hannah Arendt, "Thinking and Moral Considerations: A Lecture," *Social Research* 38, no. 3 (1971): 426, 422.

34. The locus classicus of this critique of modernism is Lukács. See Georg Lukács, *Realism in Our Time: Literature and the Class*

Struggle, trans. Hannah Mitchell and Stanley Mitchell (London: Merlin, 1962).

35. Special thanks to Gregory Chase, who served as a respondent at the Philosophy and Literature workshop held at Duke University and addressing the topic of this volume, for helping me to see this contrast.

36. Virginia Woolf, *Mrs. Dalloway* (New York: Harcourt, 1981), 192. Hereafter page numbers will be given parenthetically in the text.

37. It should be noted that the language of religion is repeatedly disavowed in the novel; Peter at one point muses on Clarissa's "atheist religion of doing good for the sake of goodness" (78).

38. For a reading of *Mrs. Dalloway* that juxtaposes external clock time against the flow of interior life, linking the former to institutional power and social convention and the latter to "mythical grandeur," see Ricoeur, *Time and Narrative*, 2:109. Ricoeur remarks on the ruminative processes of various characters (particularly Septimus and Peter) but does not explore the concept.

39. One possible exception is perhaps Clarissa's thinking about Sally Seton, her recognition through sustained attention of the enduring and extraordinary nature of her feeling for Sally, its "purity" and "integrity" (34).

40. For a useful elaboration of Murdoch's thinking along these lines, especially as it relates to dominant frameworks within moral philosophy, see Cora Diamond, "Murdoch the Explorer," *Philosophical Topics* 38, no. 1 (2010): 51–85.

41. Iris Murdoch, *The Sovereignty of Good* (New York: Routledge), 79. Hereafter page numbers will be given parenthetically in the text.

42. For a careful elaboration of the notion of attention with respect to ordinary practices of reading literature, including a discussion of Murdoch, see Toril Moi, *Revolution of the Ordinary: Literary Studies after Wittgenstein, Austin, and Cavell* (Chicago: University of Chicago Press, 2017), 227–31.

Made in the USA
Middletown, DE
23 June 2023

33256480R00099